OCR Anthology for Classical Greek GCSE 2027–2028

The following titles are available from Bloomsbury for the OCR specifications in Latin and Greek

Cicero *pro Roscio Amerino*: A Selection, with introduction, commentary notes and vocabulary by Neil Treble

OCR Anthology for Latin AS and A Level Shorter Prose Authors, covering the prescribed texts by Nepos, Tacitus and Apuleius, with introduction, commentary notes and vocabulary by Katharine Radice and Stuart R. Thomson

OCR Anthology for Latin AS and A Level Shorter Verse Authors, covering the prescribed texts by Lucretius, Tibullus and Ovid, with introduction, commentary notes and vocabulary by John Godwin

OCR Anthology for Latin GCSE 2027–2028, covering the prescribed texts by Pliny the Younger, Aulus Gellius, Apuleius, Ovid and Virgil, with introduction, commentary notes and vocabulary by Tim Chambers and Declan Lawell

OCR Anthology for Classical Greek GCSE 2027–2028, covering the prescribed texts by Herodotus, Lysias, Homer and Euripides, with introduction, commentary notes and vocabulary by Chris Burnand and Andy Mylne

OCR Anthology for Classical Greek AS and A Level: 2026–2028, covering the prescribed texts by Aristophanes, Herodotus, Homer, Lucian, Plato and Sophocles, with introduction, commentary notes and vocabulary by Matthew Barr, John Claughton, Benedict Gravell, Rowena Hewes, Ellice Hetherington and Stuart R. Thomson

Virgil *Aeneid* IV: A Selection, with introduction, commentary notes and vocabulary by John Storey

Supplementary resources for these volumes can be found at
https://bloomsbury.pub/OCReditions-2026-2028
Please type the URL into your web browser and follow the instructions to access the Companion Website. If you experience any problems, please contact Bloomsbury at onlineresources@bloomsbury.com

OCR Anthology for Classical Greek GCSE 2027–2028

Edited by
Chris Burnand and Andy Mylne

BLOOMSBURY ACADEMIC
LONDON · NEW YORK · OXFORD · NEW DELHI · SYDNEY

BLOOMSBURY ACADEMIC
Bloomsbury Publishing Plc
50 Bedford Square, London, WC1B 3DP, UK
1385 Broadway, New York, NY 10018, USA
29 Earlsfort Terrace, Dublin 2, Ireland

BLOOMSBURY, BLOOMSBURY ACADEMIC and the Diana logo are trademarks of
Bloomsbury Publishing Plc

First published in Great Britain 2025

Copyright © Chris Burnand and Andy Mylne, 2025

Christopher Burnand and Andy Mylne have expressed their right under the Copyright,
Designs and Patents Act, 1988, to be identified as Authors of this work.

Cover design: Terry Woodley
Cover image: Migfoto/Adobe Stock

All rights reserved. No part of this publication may be reproduced or transmitted in any
form or by any means, electronic or mechanical, including photocopying, recording, or any
information storage or retrieval system, without prior permission in writing from the publishers.

Bloomsbury Publishing Plc does not have any control over, or responsibility for, any
third-party websites referred to or in this book. All internet addresses given in this book
were correct at the time of going to press. The author and publisher regret any inconvenience
caused if addresses have changed or sites have ceased to exist, but can accept no
responsibility for any such changes.

A catalogue record for this book is available from the British Library.

A catalog record for this book is available from the Library of Congress.

ISBN: PB: 978-1-3503-8453-8
        ePDF: 978-1-3503-8454-5
        eBook: 978-1-3503-8455-2

Typeset by RefineCatch Limited, Bungay, Suffolk
Printed and bound in India

To find out more about our authors and books visit www.bloomsbury.com
and sign up for our newsletters.

CONTENTS

Preface 7
Introduction 8
How to Use This Book 12
Discussing Literary Style 14
Map of the Ancient Mediterranean 16
Timeline 18

Herodotus 19

Lysias 38

Homer 57

Euripides 79

OCR Greek GCSE Defined Vocabulary List 101

Endorsement statement

The teaching content of this resource is endorsed by OCR for use with specification GCSE Classical Greek (9-1) (J292).

All references to assessment, including assessment preparation and practice questions of any format/style, are the publisher's interpretation of the specification and are not endorsed by OCR.

This resource was designed for use with the version of the specification available at the time of publication. However, as specifications are updated over time, there may be contradictions between the resource and the specification, therefore please use the information on the latest specification and Sample Assessment Materials at all times when ensuring students are fully prepared for their assessments.

Endorsement indicates that a resource is suitable to support delivery of an OCR specification, but it does not mean that the endorsed resource is the only suitable resource to support delivery, or that it is required or necessary to achieve the qualification.

OCR recommends that teachers consider using a range of teaching and learning resources based on their own professional judgement for their students' needs. OCR has not paid for the production of this resource, nor does OCR receive any royalties from its sale. For more information about the endorsement process, please visit the OCR website.

PREFACE

We are delighted that Bloomsbury continues to publish books to support the study of the set texts for GCSE Classical Greek. We are particularly grateful to Judith Affleck and Clive Letchford, who established the format of these books when the new specification was first introduced, in an attempt to support pupils as they grappled with real Greek literature for the first time. They have also been kind enough to allow us to adapt the material they produced for the introductory pages of previous volumes.

Like them, we are aware of pressures on time in schools, especially if Greek does not occupy a full place in the curriculum. The Classical languages are unique in expecting GCSE pupils to study literature in the original, as part of the qualification. This is a significant step in terms of the difficulty of the challenge that it poses, but it is also a moment of the greatest excitement, as pupils are able to read for the first time the actual words composed by ancient Greeks. We hope that this textbook will provide help with the challenges involved so that pupils may be able to work independently on the texts, but also that it will help to foster the excitement of reading such authors as Homer for the first time. Indeed, we even hope that it may prove useful not only as a GCSE textbook but also as a post-GCSE reader.

As well as setting the texts in the relevant context and encouraging students to think about their content, we also have the aim to connect these texts to the GCSE language learning that pupils are also engaged with. Therefore, we follow our predecessors' practice in listing on each page those words which are set as part of the prescribed GCSE list. In addition, as we want to encourage active engagement with unfamiliar vocabulary, the notes include some derivations and connections to words on the prescribed GCSE list; this is to reinforce word-recognition, a skill fundamental at any stage of learning to read Greek. We have also made stylistic commentaries freely available on the companion website, as well as a fairly literal translation of all four texts (supplementary resources for these volumes can be found at www.bloomsbury.com/OCR-editions).

These four texts all offer a great deal of interest and we hope pupils will get as much enjoyment out of studying them as we have had in preparing them for this book.

This volume is dedicated with great gratitude to all the teachers who opened our eyes and minds to the delights of reading ancient literature.

Chris Burnand
Andy Mylne

INTRODUCTION

Greek literature spans a vast period of time, from the dawn of Greek writing through the Archaic, Classical and Hellenistic periods of Greek history and on into the Byzantine Empire and the eventual fall of Byzantium in 1453 CE. The texts in this volume come from a relatively short historical period of about 350 years, from the epic poetry of Homer in the late eighth century to Lysias who was writing his speeches in the late fifth and early fourth centuries BCE.

The following historical outline is to help set your GCSE texts in their broad context. Dates are BCE, unless otherwise stated.

Age of heroes

The Mediterranean landscape has plentiful traces of an ancient past typified by huge 'Cyclopean' walls, and palaces with great hearths, colourful wall paintings, and rooms full of storage jars, some with lists of their contents. The beginning of Greek culture goes back even earlier, as the figure of a minstrel from one of the islands around Greece carved in smooth white stone in the third millennium testifies, but it was to the Mycenaean period in particular (*c.* 1600–1200) that the Greek poets looked back. What they saw was an age of warriors in chariots, armed with bronze, valuing material possessions and honour in almost equal measure, living in palaces with great halls, where bards performed their songs and where, after death, men were buried or cremated with precious or highly crafted objects.

Colonization, Homer and the Greek alphabet

This Mycenaean palace culture collapsed at about the time that the legendary sack of Troy was believed to have taken place, dated to the start of the twelfth century by ancient scholars, such as the Alexandrian librarian Eratosthenes. A technological shift from using bronze to iron followed, one of many discoveries of the 'Dark Age' (*c.* 1150–800), so-called because relatively little is known of it. This was the beginning of a period of exploration and colonization beginning with the settlement by Greeks of the eastern Aegean in the eleventh century but extending all over the Mediterranean and Black Sea from the eighth century. Individual city-states became competitive, displaying their wealth through building projects, such as an early temple of Artemis at Ephesus, or sporting events, such as the Olympic Games, traditionally inaugurated in 776. Establishing trade links and settlements led to contact with other cultures and new ideas: for example, law codes were created and Phoenician letters were adapted to create a versatile new Greek alphabet. **The Homeric poems** emerged during this period from the now well-established Greek settlements on the Aegean coast of Turkey. Contact with more sophisticated cultures in Egypt and the Middle East continued to produce new artistic discoveries, a wealth of stories about the gods and ideas about religion, astronomy and mathematics – ideas which permeated and shaped Greek art, literature and thought.

The rise of Persia

This contact also brought a threat to Greek independence, particularly along the western coast of modern Turkey. Cities like the highly cultured Miletus came under repeated attack and eventually became subject to the Persian king Cyrus the Great. The so-called 'Archaic Period' (*c.* 800–480) ends with the Persian Wars, when the huge forces of Persia and her subject allies crossed into Greece and destroyed Athens – but were then repelled. Our main source for this conflict was a Greek from Halicarnassus, called **Herodotus**. He explores the conflict between the Greek-speaking and 'barbarian' (non-Greek-speaking) worlds, which began with the 'Ionian revolt' in 499 against Persian rule and ended, unexpectedly, with Persian defeat twenty years later. In investigating this clash of cultures and power, he traces the rise of Persia in the sixth century under Cyrus the Great and his successors, Cambyses, Darius and Xerxes. His research not only takes him back in time, but all over the known world from the fabulous wealth of Croesus, King of Lydia, to the ancient records of Egypt, the unique customs of India and, of course, to Greece. It is from Herodotus, writing in the mid-fifth century, that we get a vivid picture of the emerging characters of Greek city states and their different forms of government: the prosperous tyrannies of wealthy states like Samos, Corinth and Sicyon, the oligarchy of Sparta with its military discipline, and Athens, whose discovery of silver in Attica enabled her to establish democracy and develop a navy strong enough to help defeat the Persians.

Athens and Sparta

The Athenian historian Thucydides writes of these two city states that there was nothing lasting in the physical remains of Sparta that would lead future generations to suspect its power, whereas the impression Athens produced was of a city twice as powerful as it really was. Athens had grown in confidence, power and ambition since the Persian Wars. A successful defensive alliance against further threat from Persia to the Greeks in the Aegean, which had its treasury on Delos, was gradually transformed into an empire to benefit Athens: an empire that generated huge wealth and power for the city which came to see the cities of the original alliance as politically and militarily subject to it. Under the leadership of the great Athenian statesman Pericles, a decision to preserve the 'ground-zero effect' of the Persian occupation of 479 was reversed, and Athens used its wealth (or, as some pointed out, that of its subject-allies) to beautify the Acropolis with the marble temples that still stand today. Relations between Athens, Sparta and other states like Corinth deteriorated and an uneasy cold war turned into a major conflict, known as the Peloponnesian War, that lasted from 431 to 404. Even so, during the late fifth century Athens attracted and nurtured not only great artists and architects, partly through the vision of men like Pericles, but also great thinkers and writers, many native to Athens, like the philosopher Socrates, the comic playwright Aristophanes, or the three great tragedians, Aeschylus, Sophocles and **Euripides**. Although these authors cover a range of genres, their works have common ground, centred on human nature and man's relationship with the world around him.

Myth, drama and democracy

Herodotus is typical of these radical thinkers in trying to rationalize some of the myths of the remote past. Regardless of their veracity or chronology, Greek myths continued to provide fertile ground for exploring contemporary themes. The story of the siege and fall of Troy lay at the heart of many, and **Euripides**, for example, focused upon the experience of the women of Troy, on the beach in front of their burning city and soon to be enslaved to their Greek conquerors, to fashion a picture of the tragedy of the victims of war. Not only does this presentation hold universal relevance and resonate powerfully with the experience of similar victims of contemporary conflict, but it also may be seen to carry a warning to the dangerous over-confidence of victorious cities like Athens herself. One function of the playwrights of ancient Athens, both tragic and comic, was seen to be as teachers of the citizens, stirring them out of complacency, and developing their powers of understanding and critical thinking. This process was further enabled because Athenian theatrical performances reached audiences on an unprecedented scale; there was an appetite for debate and civic education. Athens was a city where engagement and debate were central to the political and legal processes. In the Assembly, the executive body of Athenian democracy, (male) citizens would gather in huge numbers, the size of a football crowd, to make crucial decisions, like the fatal vote to help the Ionians in 499, where Herodotus comments drily on how it was easier to persuade 30,000 Athenians than one Spartan, or the foolish optimism with which they sent a full military expedition 500 miles to Sicily while peace with Sparta was still fragile. For Athens, this decision contributed to her fall: the war ended in submission on Spartan terms. Thucydides was the historian who documented the war between Athens and Sparta and the catastrophic Sicilian Expedition until his account breaks off in 411. It was another Athenian writer, Xenophon, who recounted the dismantling of Athens' democracy and empire that came with the war's end and Athens' defeat in 404.

Athenian oratory

This defeat had significant political repercussions within Athens, as the Spartans set up a short-lived tyranny there under the so-called Thirty, before the swift reemergence of democracy. The killing of his brother by the Thirty to raise funds may in part have led **Lysias** into a new career writing speeches for plaintiffs in the Athenian courts. He was one of many orators whose speeches survive from the fourth century in both political and legal contexts. These speeches reinforce the histories of Herodotus, Thucydides and Xenophon in placing the role of oratory at the heart of Athenian democracy. Political figures such as Pericles in the fifth century and Demosthenes in the fourth had to be able to persuade the citizens in the assembly to adopt their policies: there were no political parties in Athens and each time a politician wanted something done he had to stand up and win over a majority of the citizens present at that particular assembly meeting. Similarly, in the Athenian courts, large juries heard cases, whether concerned with private law or big political cases, and the plaintiffs had to be able to speak in person to win over the hundreds of fellow citizens who were the jurors, even if, as we shall see, they could hire an expert speechwriter. These legal cases also offer a fascinating insight into aspects of Athenian life, such as the treatment and experience of slaves and women, that are hardly touched upon by narrowly political historians such as Thucydides.

The Hellenistic world

Sixty-six years after their defeat at the hands of Sparta in 404, the Athenians once again lost their independence at the Battle of Chaeronea, this time to Macedon, a newly powerful kingdom in the north of Greece. Two years later, after Philip II of Macedon was assassinated, his son Alexander the Great pursued a greater ambition: the conquest of the Persian Empire. Alexander's extraordinary victories took him and his army near the edges of the known world, deep into the deserts of Egypt, through the vast kingdom that the Persian kings had united and further east, through the Hindu Kush to India. These conquests had a lasting impact in spite of Alexander's brief life (356–323): Greek was adopted as the language of Alexander's new Hellenistic world, texts were gathered together, catalogued and annotated by scholars in the great new library at Alexandria, and Greek was spoken, written and read throughout the Roman and Byzantine periods – until the conquest of Constantinople by the Ottoman Turks in 1453 CE.

Texts

The survival of these texts over the turbulent centuries was tenuous. For a long period in European history some manuscripts were preserved in mediaeval monasteries, but almost no-one understood Greek: Petrarch, a fourteenth-century CE Italian poet, owned and treasured a Greek text of Homer but was unable to read it. In the early fifteenth century, Greek-speaking scholars, fleeing the spread of the Ottoman Empire, arrived in Italy along with their learning and libraries of manuscripts. The invention of printing in the mid-fifteenth century and of a Greek typeface created by the Aldine Press in Venice meant that access to Herodotus, Euripides, Homer and Lysias, as well as the Greek New Testament, became more widespread by the start of the sixteenth century among the wealthy elite. In England, for example, Edward VI learned enough Greek to enjoy writing it. Those who taught him and his sister Elizabeth helped introduce Greek into schools, some of which have taught it continuously since then. Today you can access almost any ancient Greek text at the touch of a key and there are more opportunities than ever to develop your knowledge of Greek, in summer schools, at university, through books or online.

HOW TO USE THIS BOOK

Starting to read a literary text is always a challenging step. This book tries to guide you into doing this confidently in a number of ways:

1. There are three levels of **introduction**:

    i) Introduction, p.8 An overview of how your texts fit into the wider picture of the history and culture of Ancient Greece.
    ii) A more specific introduction to your author or genre. In the case of Homer, this includes an introduction to his language; there is also a brief introduction to the poetic language of Greek tragedy in the Euripides section.
    iii) '**The story so far . . .**' to help you set the extract you are reading in context, so that you know what is going on. At the end of your text there may also be a '**What happens next**' section, if the story continues.

    Other reference pages you may find useful include tips for how to discuss literary style, a timeline, a map, and the GCSE word list at the back.

2. **Text and Notes**

    Each double page of text and notes contains the following:

    i) A brief heading in *italics* at the top gives an overview for that page of text.
    ii) **Names and Places, Topics and Questions**: these are to help you understand and enjoy the text. Many of the questions are genuinely open with no straightforwardly 'correct' answer.
    iii) On each double page there is a list of words from the set GCSE vocabulary relevant to the text.

    - If you have already learned the GCSE vocabulary, use this to revise from before you translate.
    - If you are still working on the GCSE vocabulary list, look these words up before you begin.

    iv) Vocabulary and translation help is arranged line by line.

    - Help with GCSE words may be given, especially if they have a slightly different meaning from the one you are used to or are used in a less familiar form.

HOW TO USE THIS BOOK

- New words that have appeared already may not be translated, but you may be directed back by a line reference to an earlier usage.
- Greek words taken directly from the text are in bold.
- The following symbols are used:

  > This means the Greek word is derived from or related to a more familiar or simple Greek word (given in blue). This is to help you understand its root meaning and perhaps remember it more easily.

  < This means that an English word is derived from the Greek. We have included some rather obscure examples, but hope to invite discussion or investigation; again, some may prove memorable.

  = This is used where a less familiar word is synonymous with (i.e. has the same meaning as) one you may already know or recognise.

You can also access a fairly literal translation on the parallel open-access website (supplementary resources for these volumes can be found at www.bloomsbury.com/OCR-editions).

Useful books

Montanari, F. (2015) *The Brill Dictionary of Ancient Greek*.
Morwood, J. (ed.) (2001) *Oxford Grammar of Classical Greek*, Oxford University Press.
Morwood, J. and Taylor, J. (eds) (2002) *Pocket Oxford Classical Greek Dictionary*, Oxford University Press.
Scott, R. and Liddell, H. G. (eds) (2010) *Intermediate Greek–English Lexicon*, Oxford University Press.
Taylor, J. (2016) *Greek to GCSE Parts 1 and 2*, 2nd edition, Bloomsbury.
Taylor, J. (2017) *Greek Beyond GCSE*, 2nd edition, Bloomsbury.

Useful editions for teachers

Lysias: Selected Speeches (2008), ed. C. Carey (Cambridge Greek and Latin Classics, Cambridge University Press).
Homer: Odyssey I–XII (1998), ed. W. B. Stanford (BCP edition of old Macmillan edition).
A Commentary on Homer's Odyssey vol II (1995) ed. A. Heubeck and A. Hoekstra (Clarendon Paperbacks, Oxford University Press).
Euripides: Troades (2019), ed. D. Kovacs (Oxford University Press).

DISCUSSING LITERARY STYLE

You have probably been used to commenting on the style of English writers, especially poets. Greek authors use similar techniques and you should be ready to comment on the style as well as the content of your set texts. If you can translate and understand the significance of the text, this should not present too much of a problem. A key difference between English and Greek is word order, which is much more flexible in Greek. Because Greek and Latin, unlike English, are inflected languages, classical authors can arrange words in a variety of ways to alter the emphasis, while keeping the same basic meaning.

You can find much more stylistic commentary on each of the four separate texts on the parallel open-access website (supplementary resources for these volumes can be found at www.bloomsbury.com/OCR-editions). However, the following paragraphs set out some ways of analysing style. The technical terms are a useful short-cut for describing what a writer is doing, but there is no substitute for properly understanding the content. Your first step when preparing for this type of discussion or exam question is to make sure you consider why the author is writing, what he has to say and how he expresses himself (almost all authors surviving from the ancient world are male writers).

One useful way to think about style is to ask yourself how the author could have expressed himself most simply, and then to consider why he has chosen to elaborate his point in particular ways. There is often no right or wrong answer, and effects may be subtle, so be prepared to engage in discussion with your fellow students and teacher. Writers on literature have developed technical vocabulary to help describe some literary effects. Before setting out a few of these terms, it is worth emphasising that as well as identifying an effect, it is important that you explain how it enhances the meaning.

1. Choice of words

An author makes many choices: for example, selecting one from a number of words with the same basic meaning (synonyms), or including words, especially adjectives and adverbs, which may not be strictly necessary. This selection is sometimes termed diction (from the Latin *dico* – I say) or lexis (from λέγω).

2. Word order

When you start learning Greek, you get used to a fairly predictable word order, often involving a nominative at the start, and a verb at the end of the clause. Unusual word order is likely to be significant. For example, has an action been emphasised by promoting the verb (moving it forward) or placing it first? Has the subject been delayed, exciting suspense in the reader? Try to read or re-read the Greek words as they come – how is the picture being built up, word-by-word? Since the lines in verse set texts (unlike prose texts) are fixed, you might also consider emphasis through position – for example, a word being delayed to the next line ('enjambment') or coming first in a line.

3. Sound

alliteration – repeated consonantal sounds (e.g. 'π', 'κ' etc) may draw a group of words together more tightly. In Greek this includes repeated sounds in any position in the word, not just at the start of a word. Listen out for the two different sounds in the double letters ζ, ξ and ψ and remember that the aspirates θ, φ and χ can be alliterative with τ, π and κ respectively.

assonance – similar to alliteration but refers to repeated vowel sounds rather than consonants.

onomatopoeia – where the sound of the word mirrors the meaning.

rhythm – verse authors (Homer and Euripides in this selection) composed following a metrical framework; rhythm may be used flexibly to underline sense.

4. Other literary terms

anaphora – a word is repeated at the start of successive clauses to give emphasis to an idea.

asyndeton – omission of conjunctions, often to speed up the narrative.

balance/contrast (antithesis) – Greek is fond of contrasting ideas, which it may signpost by using μέν and δέ.

chiasmus – a mirrored arrangement of words, reversing a word order, for example: nominative, accusative, accusative, nominative (A-B-B-A).

enjambment – a term used only in verse, where the sense runs over from one line to the next giving special emphasis to the word starting the new line.

epithet – used particularly in Homer of adjectives or phrases attached to a particular character or noun.

juxtaposition – placing of two words next to each other to bring out clearly the contrast between them.

metaphor – a situation is described using language which is not literally the case, e.g. 'on fire with love'.

repetition – words are repeated to give additional emphasis to an important idea.

pleonasm – repeating the same idea in two near synonymous words or phrases to emphasise it.

simile – where a situation or event is described as being like something else.

A good starting point for further consideration is Morwood's *Oxford Grammar of Classical Greek*, which gives examples.

MAP OF THE ANCIENT

MEDITERRANEAN

TIMELINE

Bronze Age	2500	Great pyramids built at Giza in Egypt. Development of Greek island culture and Cycladic art.
	2000–1200	1700: Minoan palace civilisation flourished on Crete. 1450: Mycenaean palace civilisation in Greece.
	1184	Traditional date for the fall of Troy, calculated by Eratosthenes.
Iron Age	1150–800	Migrations into Greece and across the Aegean. Period of colonisation; growing contact with neighbouring powers.
Archaic Greece c. 800–479	700s	776: First Olympic Games. Alphabet adopted to write Greek. *Iliad* and *Odyssey* composed.
	c. 550	Cyrus defeats the Medes and begins the establishment of the Persian Empire.
	546	Defeat of Croesus, king of Lydia, by Cyrus the Great.
	546–527	Pisistratus, tyrant of Athens. Texts of *Iliad* and *Odyssey* standardised.
	510	Hippias, son of Pisistratus, driven from Athens.
	508/7	Cleisthenes' reforms in Athens begin to establish a democratic constitution.
	499–494	The Ionian Revolt. Sack of Sardis by Ionians and Athenians.
	490	Darius invades Attica; Athenian victory at Marathon. 480s: births of **Herodotus** and **Euripides**.
	480	Xerxes' invasion of Greece; Persian victory at Thermopylae; sack of Athens; Greek naval victory at Salamis; Xerxes' retreat.
	479	Final defeat of Persians at Plataea and Mycale.
Classical Greece c. 479–323	478	Formation of the Delian League; growing tensions between Athens, Sparta and their allies.
	c. 459–445	Birth of **Lysias**.
	447	Pericles' building programme on the Acropolis begins.
	431–404	The Peloponnesian War between Athens and Sparta.
	415	First production of *Troades*.
	415–413	Athens' unsuccessful expedition to Sicily.
	404	Defeat of Athens by Sparta; establishment of Thirty Tyrants in Athens.
	403	Reestablishment of Athenian democracy; **Lysias** prosecutes Eratosthenes for the murder of his brother; **Lysias** embarks on his career as a legal speechwriter.
	338	Victory of Philip II of Macedon over the allied Greek city-states at Chaeronea.
	334–323	Conquest of the Persian Empire by Alexander the Great.

Herodotus

Herodotus was acclaimed as the 'Father of history' by the Roman politician and writer Cicero since he was the first exponent of the literary form which we (like Cicero) speak of as 'history', but to Herodotus such a title was meaningless. Before him there was no examination, written in prose, of events of the past which could claim such a title, no attempt to explore causation of such events over an extended period of time, and no notion of what the 'right way' to undertake such a task might be. What there was of course were the epic poems of Homer – orally composed narratives in verse that were certainly recounting the 'past', and were considered by their audience to be a record of real events. But these were narratives which featured men far stronger and more 'heroic' than contemporaries could aspire to be, gods openly interacting with one another, and with mortals, to affect the outcome of events in their world, and long sequences of spoken discourse that expressed the inner motivation and emotion of individual characters, much as a theatrical drama might. It is no surprise therefore that Herodotus owed much to Homer and to narrative with a very strong oral character. It has been suggested that he too delivered sections of his work as a reading or performance to an audience.

But, unlike Homer, the work of Herodotus is one that he wrote rather than composed orally, in prose rather than in verse, and with no claim to be the mouthpiece for divine inspiration. Herodotus' work was composed in nine books and was about a great conflict between East and West, the Persian Wars of 490–479, famous for events like the battles of Marathon, Thermopylae and Salamis. In this conflict, the Persian attempt to gain a foothold in Europe ended in a spectacular and unexpected victory for the Greeks. Herodotus' work is not simply the patriotic celebration such a Greek victory might justify: he is interested in the ἔργα μεγάλα τε καὶ θωμαστά, '*great and amazing deeds*', of both Greeks and non-Greeks (barbarians). Herodotus' stories have a strong moral aspect to them. Acts of injustice generate an appropriate consequence, even long after the original wrong was committed, and often in ways that are only properly appreciable in the light of hindsight. Herodotus is keen to make the cycle of the rise and fall of great men and their cities clear. It is a world where gods operate as well as men, just as in Homer, but the spirit of enquiry which drives his work forward is marked by human curiosity typical of fifth-century Greek thought.

Herodotus travelled widely and recorded traditions from a range of countries – his own boundless curiosity is a defining and appealing aspect of his work. Book 2, for example, is devoted to an account of Egypt and we hear how Herodotus questioned Egyptian priests during his travels and recorded what he learned. His research, 'ἱστορίη' in Greek, gives us both our word 'history' and the title of his work, *The Histories*. Herodotus makes great use of digressions and stories in his

Histories to amplify his over-arching themes of Greeks versus non-Greeks, liberty and slavery, and the reversal of fortune of both individuals and empires. He arranges his account artfully, sometimes putting stories with contrasting messages next to each other, but he leaves it to the reader or listener to make their own connections. The *Histories* climax in Books 8 and 9 with the Persian invasion of Greece in 480–479 and its ultimate failure, but he begins his tale by considering the origins and rapid growth of the Persian Empire. The extracts you will read are taken from Books 1 and 9.

2027–28 Prescription

This selection corresponds to **Tales from Herodotus**, *ed. Farnell and Goff.*
Section 6: How Arion was saved by a dolphin (Herodotus 1.24)
Section 7: The story of Euenius (Herodotus 9.93–4)
Section 10: Respect for suppliants enforced by an oracle (Herodotus 1.157–9)

The story so far

These three extracts are drawn from very different parts of Herodotus' *Histories*, the great work in which he charts the process by which the Greeks and Persians came to be at war early in the fifth century BCE. But they each demonstrate characteristics typical of Herodotus' style of narration.

First, they take the form of self-contained anecdotes which crop up in the course of Herodotus' main narrative: their immediate relevance to the narrative from which they emerge varies, but clearly what motivates Herodotus to include them is that he enjoys them and thinks them worthy of passing on to his reader. Secondly, to a greater or lesser degree, they demonstrate the workings of powers beyond normal human experience: powers that are manifest in the world in which mortals live and which often shape mortal lives and experience, but which they struggle to explain or comprehend fully.

In the first, a famous musician, Arion, is miraculously saved from what seems inevitable death at the hands of thugs, and his assailants are later forced to confess their evil designs. Herodotus, as a literary artist, clearly enjoys the fact that Arion's artistry saves him, but, as throughout his work, it is also important to him to show that injustice is exposed. In the other two passages, Herodotus is apparently attracted by the mysterious and sometimes counter-intuitive ways that justice overseen by the gods operates in the world of men. Once again in the story of Euenius, as in that of Arion, deceit and the dispensation of justice both feature. But Herodotus reveals that the way that mortals take the process of justice into their own hands does not necessarily conform to what the gods see as the appropriate response. This idea is taken still further in the third passage: the people of Cyme are put in a challenging moral and political situation by the arrival of Pactyes, a fugitive from the Persians, who is demanding his god-protected right to asylum as a suppliant. Are they to appease the Persian aggressors who are ordering them to surrender Pactyes and ignore the divine protection afforded to a fugitive? Or should they honour a suppliant's rightful claim for protection but then face the consequences of their actions at the hands of the Persians? They view their attempts to gain clarity on the matter from the god Apollo as a sensible thing to do, but the god sees things differently: their attempt at piety is actually a demonstration of impiety – they should have known what to do, but were distracted by the mortal, political considerations involved in their dilemma. This story has, in our own times, gained a relevance that spans the centuries, as the countries of Europe have also had to confront the competing claims of morality and politics in decisions on how to respond to the needs of immigrants who have claimed asylum with them.

Figure 1 *Third-century* CE *mosaic depicting Arion riding a dolphin. From Henchir Thyna (ancient city of Thaenae), the Baths, Tunisia.*
Photo by DEA PICTURE LIBRARY/De Agostini via Getty Images.

How Arion was saved by a dolphin

Arion, a famous musician, is on his way home to Corinth, having become wealthy from a tour of southern Italy and Sicily, but is assaulted by a group of fellow Corinthians.

Ἀρίων ὁ κιθαρῳδός, τὸν πολὺν τοῦ χρόνου διατρίβων παρὰ Περιάνδρῳ τῷ Κορίνθου τυράννῳ, ἐπεθύμησε πλεῦσαι εἰς Ἰταλίαν τε καὶ Σικελίαν. ἐργασάμενος δὲ χρήματα μεγάλα, ἠθέλησεν ὀπίσω εἰς Κόρινθον ἀφικέσθαι. ὡρμᾶτο μέν νυν ἐκ Τάραντος, πιστεύων δὲ οὐδαμοῖς μᾶλλον ἢ   5
Κορινθίοις, ἐμισθώσατο πλοῖον ἀνδρῶν Κορινθίων. οἱ δὲ ἐν τῷ πελάγει ἐπεβούλευον, τὸν Ἀρίονα ἐκβαλόντες, ἔχειν τὰ χρήματα. ὁ δέ, συνεὶς τοῦτο, ἐλίσσετο, χρήματα μὲν αὑτοῖς προϊείς, ψυχὴν δὲ παραιτούμενος. οὔκουν δὴ ἔπειθεν, ἀλλ' ἐκέλευον αὐτὸν οἱ πορθμεῖς ἢ διαχρῆσθαι   10
ἑαυτόν, ὡς ταφῆς ἐν γῇ τύχοι, ἢ ἐκπηδᾶν εἰς τὴν θάλατταν τὴν ταχίστην. ἀπειληθεὶς δὲ ὁ Ἀρίων εἰς ἀπορίαν, παρῃτήσατο αὐτοὺς περιιδεῖν αὐτὸν ἐν τῇ σκευῇ πάσῃ στάντα ἐν τοῖς ἑδωλίοις ᾆσαι· ᾄσας δὲ ὑπεδέχετο ἑαυτὸν κατεργάσεσθαι.   15

Names and places

Ἀρίων -ονος ὁ: Arion, *a semi-legendary poet and musician of the seventh century* BCE.

Ἰταλία -ας ἡ: Italy. *Much of the south and the western coast of Italy had been colonised by settlers from Greek cities like Corinth. This caused it to be referred to as 'Magna Graecia' – the Latin for 'Great Greece'. The 'mother cities' of these settlers kept close relations with their colonies in Italy.*

Κόρινθος -ου ἡ: Corinth. *The city situated on the narrow neck of land (isthmus) linking the Peloponnese and the remainder of mainland Greece. With two harbours on either shore of the isthmus, Corinth's ability to trade to the east and west gave it great wealth. Its prosperity was increased by enlightened despots such as Periander.*

Κορίνθιοι -ων οἱ: Corinthians, *inhabitants of Corinth.*

Περίανδρος -ου ὁ: Periander, *autocrat in the city of Corinth 625–585* BCE. *The Greek word* τύραννος, *from which the English 'tyrant' derives, was not necessarily negative. For many, despots like Periander brought prosperity and influence to their cities: he encouraged wider trade, both by colonisation and his close contact with other autocrats around the Greek world.*

Σικελία -ας ἡ: Sicily, *the island to the immediate south of Italy. As with Italy itself, Sicily was settled by colonists from Greek cities and was Greek speaking.*

Τάρας -αντος ὁ: Tarentum, *an important Greek city, founded by Spartan settlers, in the 'arch' of the 'boot' formed by the geographical shape of Italy.*

> **GCSE vocabulary:** ἀλλά, ἀνήρ, αὐτόν, ἀφικνέομαι, βάλλω (ἐκβαλόντες), δέ, δή, ἑαυτόν, ἐθέλω, εἰς, ἐκ, ἐν, ἔχω, ἤ, ἤ…ἤ…, θάλασσα, κελεύω, μᾶλλον, μέγας, μέν…δέ…, νῦν, οὗτος, πᾶς, πείθω, πιστεύω, πλέω, πλοῖον, πολύς, ταχύς (τάχιστος), τε…καί…, χρήματα, χρόνος.

1 κιθαρῳδός -οῦ ὁ (< guitar) – cithara player (*a cithara is a stringed instrument like a harp*), professional musician (*here*); τὸν πολύν (πολύς *with the article becomes a noun*) – the majority, a lot (of); διατρίβω (< diatribe) – spend (time).
2 παρά + *dat.* – at the court of; τύραννος -ου ὁ – tyrant (*the title of tyrant does not yet have negative implications*); ἐπιθυμέω – desire.
3 χρήματα ἐργάζομαι (> ἔργον) – make money by working.
4 ὀπίσω – back; ὁρμάομαι – set out.
5 μέν (*with no corresponding* δέ, *gives emphasis to the word before it*) – indeed; οὐδαμός -ή -όν (*an Ionian form of the more familiar Attic* οὐδείς) – nobody.
6 μισθόομαι (*aorist* ἐμισθωσάμην) – hire.
7 πέλαγος -εος τό (< archipelago) – sea; ἐπιβουλεύω (> βουλή) – plot (*NB the imperfect tense conveys the sense of 'began to …'*).
8 συνείς (*masc. nom. sing. aorist participle active of* συνίημι) – having realised; λίσσομαι – plead (*the imperfect tense again conveys the sense of 'started to …'*).
9 προϊείς (*masc. nom. sing. present participle active of* προΐημι) – hand over; ψυχή -ῆς ἡ (< psychology) – life; παραιτέομαι – beg for; οὔκουν – certainly not; δή (*emphasises the word before it*) – at all.
10 πορθμεύς -έως ὁ – sailor; διαχράομαι (> χράομαι) – kill.
11 ὡς (+ *subjunctive or, in historic sequence, + optative, introduces a purpose clause, like* ἵνα); ταφή -ῆς ἡ (< cenotaph) – burial; τύχοι (*aorist optative active* τυγχάνω) + *gen.* – gain; ἐκπηδάω – leap off, jump overboard.
12 τὴν ταχίστην (*adverbial – the noun* ὁδόν *is understood: literally 'the quickest way'*) – very speedily; ἀπειλέω – force; ἀπορία -ας ἡ – state of helplessness.
13 παρῃτήσατο – *see l.9*; περιιδεῖν (*aorist infinitive active of* περιοράω) – allow; σκευή -ῆς ἡ – finery.
14 στάντα (*masc. acc. sing. aorist participle active of* ἵστημι) – having taken up position; ἐδώλιον -ου τό – stern seat (*usually reserved for the steersman and captain*); ἆσαι (*aorist infinitive active* ᾄδω) – to sing; ἄσας (*aorist participle active of* ᾄδω); ὑποδέχομαι – promise.
15 κατεργάζομαι – do away with.

> Q. What do you suggest might have motivated Arion to leave his life in Corinth?
> Q. Suggest why Herodotus includes the detail of Arion's preference to hire a boat from his fellow Corinthians.
> Q. What impression do we get of Arion from lines 1–15?

Arion gives an impromptu recital before leaping into the sea. Whilst the treacherous sailors sail on, believing Arion has died, he is conveyed back to Corinth independently and informs Periander of what has happened.

οἱ δέ, εἰσῆλθε γὰρ αὐτοῖς ἡδονὴ εἰ μέλλοιεν ἀκούσεσθαι
τοῦ ἀρίστου ἀνθρώπων ἀοιδοῦ, ἀνεχώρησαν ἐκ τῆς
πρύμνης εἰς μέσην ναῦν. ὁ δέ, ἐνδύς τε πᾶσαν τὴν σκευὴν
καὶ λαβὼν τὴν κιθάραν, στὰς ἐν τοῖς ἑδωλίοις διεξῆλθε
νόμον τὸν ὄρθιον· τελευτῶντος δὲ τοῦ νόμου ἔρριψεν εἰς   20
τὴν θάλατταν ἑαυτὸν ὡς εἶχε σὺν τῇ σκευῇ πάσῃ.
καὶ οἱ μὲν ἀπέπλεον εἰς Κόρινθον· τὸν δὲ Ἀρίονα
δελφίς, ὥς λέγουσι, ὑπολαβὼν ἐξήνεγκεν ἐπὶ Ταίναρον.
ἀποβὰς δὲ ἐχώρει εἰς Κόρινθον σὺν τῇ σκευῇ, καὶ
ἀφικόμενος ἀφηγεῖτο πᾶν τὸ γεγονός. Περίανδρος δὲ ὑπὸ   25
ἀπιστίας Ἀρίονα μὲν ἐν φυλακῇ εἶχεν οὐδαμῇ μεθιείς,
ἀνακῶς δὲ εἶχε τῶν πορθμέων. ὡς δὲ ἄρα παρῆσαν,
κληθέντας αὐτοὺς ἤρετο εἴ τι λέγοιεν περὶ Ἀρίονος.
φαμένων δὲ ἐκείνων ὡς εἴη τε σῶς περὶ Ἰταλίαν καὶ
λίποιεν εὖ πράττοντα ἐν Τάραντι, ἐπεφάνη αὐτοῖς ὁ   30
Ἀρίων, ὥσπερ ἔχων ἐξεπήδησε. καὶ οἱ δὲ ἐκπλαγέντες
οὐκ εἶχον ἔτι ἐλεγχόμενοι ἀρνεῖσθαι.

Place

Ταίναρον -ου τό: Cape Taenarum, *the promontory at the southern tip of Laconia, the middle of the three promontories giving the south Peloponnese its distinctive shape. Arion would still have had a long way to go in his singing attire as he moved north through the whole Peloponnese, to reach Corinth.*

Ancient Greek music

Music was of great significance in public life in Ancient Greece. When it accompanied songs recounting the stories which a community inherited and shared, music was fundamental to the generation of an ancient society's sense of its common identity. In Athens, music was enjoyed as an element of public life in ancient drama, tragedy and comedy, and the large choral performances known as dithyrambs. Both featured in the festivals that were at the heart of the city's cultural, political and religious life. Among the most common virtuoso instruments played at them were the diaulos (a double flute) and the cithara and the lyre, both stringed instruments in the manner of a small harp: where the lyre was thought rather more rustic in character, the cithara was used by professional musicians like Arion who would accompany his own singing on the instrument.

- Q. What do you think was in Arion's mind as he got dressed up in his finery to stand at the stern and sing?
- Q. Why is Arion's attire stressed by Herodotus through this story?
- Q. Given what subsequently happened, why might Herodotus have identified the high-pitched character of Arion's chosen last song?
- Q. What does Herodotus' aside (ὥς λέγουσι) in l.23, suggest to you? How do Periander's actions in lines 25–8 affect your view?
- Q. What do you think of Periander's interrogation technique?

GCSE vocabulary: ἀγαθός (ἄριστος), ἀκούω, ἀναχωρέω, ἄνθρωπος, αὐτόν, ἀφικνέομαι, βαίνω (ἀποβάς), γίγνομαι (γεγονός), δέ, ἑαυτόν, εἰ, εἰς, ἐκ, ἐκεῖνος, ἐν, ἐπί, ἔρχομαι (εἰσῆλθε), ἐρωτάω, ἔτι, εὖ, ἔχω, θάλασσα, καί, καλέω (κληθέντας), λαμβάνω, λέγω, λείπω, μέλλω, μέν … δέ …, ναῦς, νόμος, οὐκ, πᾶς, περί, πλέω (ἀπέπλεον), πράττω, τε … καί …, ὑπό, φαίνομαι, ὡς.

16   οἱ δέ (*changes the subject to the sailors*) – but they; ἡδονή -ῆς ἡ – pleasure, joy; εἰ μέλλοιεν (*the present optative active after* εἰ *here has a force similar to a purpose clause*) – in the hope that they might be about to.
17   ἀοιδός -οῦ ὁ – singer.
18   πρύμνα -ης ἡ – prow; μέσος -η -ον – middle of; ἐνδύς (*masc. nom. sing. aorist participle active of* ἐνδύω) – having put on; σκευήν – finery.
19   κιθάρα -ας ἡ – cithara (see l.1); στὰς ἐν τοῖς ἑδωλίοις (see l.14); διεξῆλθε (> ἦλθον) – performed.
20   νόμον τὸν ὄρθιον (> νόμος) – a high-pitched song (*Arion performs a hymn in honour of Apollo, sung in a falsetto; the word* νόμος = law *here acknowledges the formal rhythmic structure of the song*); τελευτάω – come to an end; ῥίπτω (*aorist:* ἔρριψα) – hurl.
21   ὡς εἶχε (*impf. indicative of* ἔχω) – as he was; σύν + *dat*. – along with; σκευή – see l.18.
23   δελφίς -ῖνος ὁ (< Delphi) – dolphin; ὑπολαμβάνω – take up; ἐξήνεγκεν – *aorist of* ἐκφέρω; ἐπί + *acc*. – to.
24   ἀποβάς (> βαίνω); χωρέω – go; σύν – see l.21.
25   ἀφηγέομαι – relate; γεγονός (*neut. acc. sing. perfect participle active of* γίγνομαι, *taken with* τό) – what happened; ὑπό + *gen*. – because of.
26   ἀπιστία -ας ἡ (> πιστεύω) – disbelief; ἐν φυλακῇ (> φυλάσσω) – under guard; οὐδαμῇ – nowhere; μεθιείς (*masc. nom. sing. present participle active*) – letting him go.
27   ἀνακῶς … εἶχε + *gen*. – watched carefully for; πορθμεύς -έως ὁ – sailor (see l.10); ἄρα (*note the different accent from the interrogative particle* ἆρα) – actually; παρῆσαν (3rd plural impf. of πάρειμι) – they were present.
28   εἴ τι λέγοιεν – if they had anything to say (*the present optative form of the verb implies an element of deliberation on the part of the sailors*).
29   φαμένων (*used as the present participle of* φημί, *masc. gen. plur.*) – saying; ὡς = ὅτι (*introducing an indirect statement in historic sequence* – *with optative* εἴη – *as if after the verb* λέγω); σῶς, σῶα, σῶν (> σώζω) – safe; περί + *acc*. (*as if there is movement involved*) – wandering around.
30   λίποιεν – see εἴη l.29 (*optative in indirect statement*); ἐπιφαίνω (< epiphany) – reveal.
31   ὥσπερ ἔχων ἐξεπήδησε – just as he was when he leapt overboard; ἐκπλαγέντες (*masc. nom. plur. aorist participle passive*) – thunderstruck.
32   ἔχω + *inf*. – be able; ἐλέγχω – cross-examine; ἀρνέομαι – deny.

The story of Euenius

When sacred sheep are killed on his watch, Euenius tries unsuccessfully to cover up what has happened. He is punished by his fellow citizens but with unforeseen consequences.

ἔστιν ἐν τῇ Ἀπολλωνίᾳ ἱερὰ ἡλίου πρόβατα, ἃ τὰς
μὲν ἡμέρας βόσκεται παρὰ ποταμόν τινα, τὰς δὲ νύκτας
ᾑρημένοι ἄνδρες, οἱ πλούτῳ τε καὶ γένει δοκιμώτατοι   35
τῶν ἀστῶν, φυλάττουσιν ἐνιαυτὸν ἕκαστος· περὶ πολλοῦ
γὰρ δὴ ποιοῦνται οἱ Ἀπολλωνιᾶται τὰ πρόβατα ταῦτα
ἐκ θεοπροπίου τινός· ἐν δὲ ἄντρῳ αὐλίζονται ἀπὸ τῆς
πόλεως ἑκάς. ἔνθα δὴ τότε ὁ Εὐήνιος οὗτος ᾑρημένος
ἐφύλαττε.   40
καί ποτε αὐτοῦ κατακοιμηθέντος, λύκοι εἰς τὸ ἄντρον
εἰσελθόντες διέφθειραν τῶν προβάτων ὡς ἑξήκοντα. ὁ
δέ, ὡς ᾔσθετο, εἶχε σιγῇ καὶ ἔφραζεν οὐδενί, ἐν νῷ ἔχων
ἀντικαταστήσειν ἄλλα πριάμενος. οἱ δὲ Ἀπολλωνιᾶται
ὡς ἐπύθοντο, οὐ γὰρ ἔλαθεν αὐτοὺς ταῦτα γενόμενα,   45
ὑπαγαγόντες αὐτὸν ὑπὸ δικαστήριον κατέκριναν τῆς
ὄψεως στερηθῆναι.
ἐπεὶ δὲ τὸν Εὐήνιον ἐξετύφλωσαν, αὐτίκα μετὰ ταῦτα
οὔτε πρόβατα αὐτοῖς ἔτικτεν οὔτε γῆ ἔφερεν ὁμοίως καρπόν.

Names and places

Ἀπολλωνία -ίας ἡ: Apollonia, *a city founded by settlers from Corinth in the time of Periander and situated in southern ancient Illyria, in modern Albania, near the Adriatic sea.*

Ἀπολλωνιᾶται –ῶν οἱ: citizens of Apollonia.

Εὐήνιος -ου ὁ: Euenius, *a young nobleman placed in charge of the sacred flock of sheep.*

Shepherds and their flocks

Shepherds hold a significant place in Classical Greek literature – primarily perhaps because of Greek society's rural, herding and pastoral, origins. However, the wildness of the landscape they inhabit is often reflected in their literary character – in Homer's *Odyssey* the one-eyed giant, the Cyclops Polyphemus, reflects that wildness in his cannibalism: uncivilised urges are exhibited, too, by Paris, son of Priam, brought up as a shepherd on Mt Ida, who runs off with Helen, the wife of King Menelaus of Sparta. But, with other figures from ancient myth, like Oedipus and King Cyrus of Persia, their unique qualities stand out in stark contrast to their early life, abandoned on wild mountainsides only to be found and brought to their destiny by uneducated shepherds.

> **GCSE vocabulary:** ἄγω (ὑπαγαγόντες), αἰσθάνομαι, ἄλλος, ἀνήρ, ἀπό, αὐτόν, γάρ, γῆ, γίγνομαι, δέ, δή, διαφθείρω, εἰς, ἕκαστος, ἐν, ἐπεί, ἔρχομαι (εἰσελθόντες), ἔχω, ἡμέρα, ἱερός, καί, μέν … δέ … , μετά, νύξ, ὅς, οὐδείς, οὐ, οὔτε … οὔτε, οὗτος, παρά, πόλις, ποταμός, πυνθάνομαι, τε … καί … , σιγή, τις, τότε, ὑπό, φαίνομαι, φέρω, φυλάσσω, ὡς.

33 ἔστιν (*first word of a sentence; neut. plur. subject*) – there are; ἥλιος -ου ὁ (< heliocentric) – the sun; πρόβατα -ων τά – sheep.
34 βόσκομαι – graze (*intransitive verb: the present tenses over the next few lines denote the habitual practice of the citizens of Apollonia regarding these animals*).
35 ᾑρημένοι (*perfect participle passive of* αἱρέομαι) (> αἱρέω) – picked; πλοῦτος -ου ὁ (> πλούσιος) – wealth; γένος -ους τό – family, lineage; δόκιμος -η -ον – notable.
36 ἀστός -οῦ ὁ – citizen; ἐνιαυτός -οῦ ὁ – year; ἕκαστος (*nom. sing. with a plural verb, in apposition to* ἄνδρες *l.35*) – each one; περὶ πολλοῦ … ποιέομαι – value highly.
37 πρόβατα -ων τά – *see l.33*.
38 ἐκ + *gen.* – as a result of (*here*); θεοπρόπιον -ου τό – prophecy; ἄντρον -ου τό – cave; αὐλίζομαι – pen (*verb*).
39 ἑκάς – far away; ἔνθα – there; ᾑρημένος – *see l.35*.
41 ποτε (*without an accent is indefinite, like* τις) – at some time; κατακοιμάομαι (*aorist* κατεκοιμησάμην) – fall asleep; λύκος -ου ὁ (< lycanthrope) – wolf.
42 ὡς (*followed by a number*) – approximately; ἑξήκοντα – sixty.
43 εἶχε σιγῇ – kept quiet; φράζω (< periphrasis) – tell; ἐν νῷ ἔχω – intend.
44 ἀντικαταστήσειν (*future infinitive active of* ἀντικαθίστημι) – to substitute; πριάμενος – having bought.
45 οὐ … ἔλαθεν αὐτοὺς ταῦτα γενόμενα (λανθάνω *lit. =* escape the notice: *the verb regularly combines with a participle in this idiomatic way*) – these things had not happened without them realising.
46 ὑπαγαγόντες – having brought … to (*followed by* ὑπό + *acc.*); δικαστήριον -ου τό – (law)court; κατακρίνω – condemn.
47 ὄψις -εως ἡ – sight; στερέω + *gen.* – deprive of.
48 ἐκτυφλόω (*aorist* ἐξετύφλωσα) – make blind; αὐτίκα – immediately.
49 τίκτω – produce young; ὁμοίως (< homophone) – in the same way (as before); καρπός -οῦ ὁ (< polycarpic) – fruit, produce.

> Q. Why does Herodotus include details of the lineage and wealth of the men chosen to guard the flock overnight?
> Q. Why do you think the citizens of Apollonia responded so extremely to the death of the sheep?
> Q. What consideration might have prompted the citizens of Apollonia to think that blinding Euenius was a reasonable punishment?

The gods indicate that the Apollonians' treatment of Euenius is the cause of their problems, and that only after he has been recompensed will they reverse the Apollonians' suffering.

ἐπερωτωμένοις δὲ αὐτοῖς ἔν τε Δωδώνῃ καὶ 50
ἐν Δελφοῖς τὸ αἴτιον τοῦ παρόντος κακοῦ, τοιάδε ἔφραζον
οἱ θεοί, "ἀδίκως τὸν φύλακα τῶν ἱερῶν προβάτων
Εὐήνιον τῆς ὄψεως ἐστερήσατε· ἡμεῖς γὰρ ἐφωρμήσαμεν
τοὺς λύκους, οὐ πρότερόν τε παυσόμεθα τιμωροῦντες
ἐκείνῳ πρὶν ἂν δίκας δῶτε ἃς ἂν αὐτὸς ἕληται καὶ δικαιοῖ· 55
τούτων δὲ τελουμένων αὐτοὶ δώσομεν Εὐηνίῳ δόσιν
τοιαύτην ἣν ἔχοντα πολλοὶ ἀνθρώπων μακαριοῦσιν αὐτόν."

οἱ δὲ Ἀπολλωνιᾶται ἀπόρρητα ποιησάμενοι τὰ χρηστήρια
ταῦτα, προύθεσαν ἀστοῖς τισι διαπρᾶξαι· οἱ δὲ
αὐτοῖς διέπραξαν ὧδε· καθημένου Εὐηνίου ἐν θάκῳ, 60
ἐλθόντες παρίζοντο αὐτῷ, καὶ λόγους ἄλλους ἐποιοῦντο
εἰς ὃ κατέβαινον συλλυπούμενοι τῷ πάθει. ταύτῃ δὲ
ὑπάγοντες ἠρώτων τίνα δίκην ἂν ἕλοιτο, εἰ ἐθέλοιεν
Ἀπολλωνιᾶται δίκας ὑποστῆναι δώσειν τῶν ποιηθέντων.

Places

Δωδώνη -ης ἡ: Dodona, *the remote location in north-west Greece of one of the ancient world's most venerable oracles of Zeus. Visitors would consult the sacred oak tree at the site, perhaps by listening intently to the rustling of the leaves. The god's response would then be interpreted by the priest. Many lead tablets inscribed with the questions put by visitors survive.*

Δελφοί -ῶν οἱ: Delphi, *the location of the sanctuary of Apollo, the most famous and revered of all Greek oracles; it is located a few miles from the northern shore of the Gulf of Corinth, on the slopes of Mt Parnassus.*

Oracles

The word 'oracle' is used both of the sanctuary of the god consulted and of the response the god gives. For an Ancient Greek, consulting an oracle meant being brought as close to divinity as ever an individual would be. He believed that he was both presenting a question directly to, and receiving a response directly from, the god. It was an awesome and frightening undertaking. The authority, and essential truth, of the response would rarely be questioned: however, the fallibility of human understanding of the underlying truth was often cruelly exposed by events.

Q. What question do you imagine the Apollonians put to the gods at Dodona and Delphi?

Q. Why do you think the Apollonians put their question to the oracles at both locations?

Q. What elements of the oracular responses suggest their authority?

Q. Why might the Apollonians have been surprised by the way the gods respond to their question? How does Herodotus characterise the way they go about fulfilling the obligation imposed on them?

HERODOTUS

> **GCSE vocabulary:** ἄδικος (ἀδίκως), αἴτιος, ἄλλος, ἄν, ἄνθρωπος, αὐτός, βαίνω (κατέβαινον), γάρ, δέ, δίδωμι (δώσω), δίκαιος, ἐθέλω, εἰς, ἐκεῖνος, ἐν, ἔρχομαι (ἐλθόντες), ἐρωτάω, θεός, ἡμεῖς, ἱερός, καί, κακός, λόγος, ὅς, οὐ, οὗτος, παύω, ποιέω, πολύς, πρότερον, τε... καί..., τις, τίς, τοιοῦτος, φύλαξ.

50   ἐπερωτωμένοις (> ἐρωτάω) – enquiring (*dative participle agreeing with* αὐτοῖς, *the indirect object of* φράζω *l.51*).

51   πάρειμι – be present; τοιάδε (> τοιοῦτος) – the following (*neut. plur.*); φράζω – tell.

52   προβάτα – sheep (*see l.33*).

53   ὄψις -εως ἡ (> ὁράω) – sight, the ability to see; στερέω – deprive X (*acc.*) of Y (*gen.*); ἐφορμάω (*aorist* ἐφόρμησα) – provoke, set on.

54   πρότερον – sooner (*picked up by* πρίν *in l.55*); τε – and (*placed after* πρότερον *rather than* οὐ, *as the two words are taken so closely together*); τιμωρέω + *dat.* – avenge.

55   πρίν (+ ἄν *& subjunctive: responding to* πρότερον *in l.54*) – before such time as; δίκας δῶτε (δῶτε: *2nd plur. aorist subjunctive active, following* πρὶν ἄν) – pay the just recompense; ἃς ἄν – whatever (ἄν + *subjunctive = the indefinite construction*); ἕληται (> αἱρέω) (*aorist subjunctive middle following* ἃς ἄν) – he chooses; δικαιοῖ (*3rd sing. present subjunctive – see* ἕληται) (> δίκαιος) – he considers right.

56   τελέω (> τέλος) – accomplish; δόσις -εως ἡ (> δίδωμι) – gift.

57   ἥν (*the relative pronoun is the object of* ἔχοντα *literally = 'having which'*) – 'that for having it'; πολλοὶ ἀνθρώπων (πολλοί *here is working both as a* (*nominative*) *noun, and as a* (*masc. plural*) *adjective referring to* ἀνθρώπων) – many people; μακαριοῦσιν (*3rd plur. future indicative of* μακαρίζω) – they will consider happy.

58   ἀπόρρητα ποιησάμενοι – keeping secret; χρηστήριον -ου τό – oracle (*the plural reflects the oracular responses given by the different sanctuaries*).

59   προύθεσαν (= προ-ἔθεσαν, *3rd plur. aorist indicative of* προτίθημι: *the augment and the final vowel of the prefix contract*) + *dat.* – appointed as a task to; ἀστός -οῦ ὁ – citizen (*see l.36*); διαπράσσω (> πράσσω) – put them (the oracular responses) into practice.

60   αὐτοῖς – for them (*the 3rd plural pronoun refers to the people of Apollonia, rather than those they had assigned the task to*); ὧδε – as follows; καθήμενος -η -ον (*participle of* κάθημαι) – sitting; θᾶκος -ου ὁ – seat.

61   παρίζομαι + *dat.* – sit beside (*the imperfect tense denotes the beginning of a process*); λόγοι – a conversation (*here*).

62   εἰς ὅ – until; καταβαίνω (> βαίνω) (< katabatic) – end up (*i.e. after a long discussion they eventually 'came down' to the point they wanted to*); συλλυπέομαι + *dat.* – sympathise with; πάθος -ους τό (< pathologist) – suffering; ταύτῃ – in this way (*fem. dat. sing. of* οὗτος, *used adverbially*).

63   ὑπάγω – lead gradually on; δίκην... ἕλοιτο (*see l.55: here* ἄν, *followed by the optative mood, indicates a potential outcome, the main clause of a hypothetical condition*) – he would choose; εἰ ἐθέλοιεν – if he wanted (*optative: 'if' clause of the condition*).

64   ὑποστῆναι – to promise; δίκας... δώσειν – *see l.55*; τῶν ποιηθέντων – for the things that had been done (*an objective genitive*).

Euenius gives his response to the Apollonians' enquiry, a comparatively modest request for land and a place to live. He discovers the trick but is duly compensated with prophetic powers.

ὁ δὲ οὐκ ἀκηκοὼς τὸ θεοπρόπιον εἵλετο, εἰπὼν ὅτι εἰ 65
δοθεῖεν αὐτῷ ἀγροί τινες κάλλιστοι ὄντες τῶν ἐν τῇ
Ἀπολλωνίᾳ, καὶ οἴκησις πρὸς τούτοις, ἣν ᾔδει καλλίστην
οὖσαν τῶν ἐν πόλει, τὸ λοιπὸν ἀμήνιτος ἂν εἴη, καὶ αὕτη
ἡ δίκη ἂν ἀποχρῴη. καὶ ὁ μὲν ταῦτα ἔλεγεν, οἱ δὲ
πάρεδροι εἶπον ὑπολαβόντες, "Εὐήνιε, ταύτην τὴν δίκην 70
Ἀπολλωνιᾶται τῆς ἐκτυφλώσεως ἐκτίνουσι κατὰ
θεοπρόπια τὰ γενόμενα."
ὁ μὲν δὴ πρὸς ταῦτα δεινὰ ἐποιεῖτο, ἐντεῦθεν πυθόμενος
τὸν πάντα λόγον, ὡς ἐξαπατηθείς· οἱ δὲ διδόασιν αὐτῷ
ἃ εἵλετο. καὶ μετὰ ταῦτα αὐτίκα ἔμφυτον μαντικὴν 75
εἶχεν ὥστε καὶ ὀνομαστὸς γενέσθαι.

Prophets and prophetesses

The status of those with prophetic (mantic) skills in Ancient Greece was often conflicted and reflected the awkward place that a prophet had in a community, bridging the world of the divine and that of mortals. Such people often are portrayed as living on the edges of society and are treated with only grudging respect. Cassandra, the daughter of king Priam of Troy, was granted the ability to tell the future by Apollo, but he doomed her also never to be believed. This tension between knowledge and disbelief is a feature of the portrayal of prophets in Classical literature. Most famously, the mantic skill of the prophet Teiresias is met by the angry suspicion of the kings to whom he delivers difficult truths in Sophocles' plays 'Oedipus the King' and 'Antigone'. He is mocked for his blindness and accused of conspiracy but, in both cases, he is shown to have told things as they are and will be. This association between physical blindness and prophetic 'sight' is also exhibited in the story of Euenius.

Figure 2 *Bronze statuette of a shepherd, Greek, c. 525–500* BCE. *Shepherds and their flocks were often a symbol of simple rural life in ancient Greek art: however, Euenius' position as overseer of the sacred flock at Apollonia was not a measure of poverty or being on the edge of society, but rather reflected his high status within this community.*
Photo: Metropolitan Museum of Art 43.11.3, Rogers Fund, 1943.

> **GCSE vocabulary:** ἀγρός, ἀκούω (ἀκηκοώς), ἄν, αὐτόν, γίγνομαι, δέ, δεινός, δίδωμι (δοθεῖεν, διδόασιν), εἰ, εἰμί, ἔχω, καί, καλός, κατά, λέγω, μέν… δέ…, μετά, οἶδα (ᾔδει), ὅς, ὅτι, οὗτος, πᾶς, ποιέω, πόλις, πυνθάνομαι, τις, ὥστε.

65   ὁ δέ – *changes the subject to Euenius*; ἀκηκοώς (*perfect participle of* ἀκούω) – having heard; θεοπρόπιον -ου τό – oracular response; εἵλετο – (*see l.55: aorist middle indicative*) chose, made his choice.

66   δοθεῖεν – *aorist optative passive of* δίδωμι: *the optative replaces indicative in an indirect statement after* ὅτι *in historic sequence*; τῶν – (*refers to* ἀγρῶν *understood*) of those.

67   οἴκησις -εως ἡ (< synoecism) – dwelling; πρός + *dat.* – in addition to; ᾔδει (*3rd sing. past of* οἶδα) – he knew.

68   οὖσαν (*participle in indirect statement after verb of knowing*) – to be; τῶν – (*see l.66: refers to* οἰκήσεων *understood*) of those; τὸ λοιπόν – (*used adverbially*) thereafter, in the future; ἀμήνιτος -ον – free of resentment; ἂν εἴη (*see l.63 – the potential construction*) – he would be.

69   δίκη -ης ἡ – recompense (*see l.55*); ἀποχρῷη (*3rd sing. present optative active; potential optative after* ἄν *see l.63*) – would be sufficient.

70   πάρεδρος -ον – sitting beside (him); ὑπολαμβάνω – reply; δίκη – *see l.55*.

71   ἐκτύφλωσις -εως ἡ – blinding; ἐκτίνω – pay in full (*followed by acc. of the thing paid and gen. of the thing paid for*).

72   θεοπρόπιον – *see l.65*; τὰ γενόμενα – (*here*) which have been made.

73   πρός + *acc.* (*governing* ταῦτα) – in response to (*here*); δεινὰ ἐποιεῖτο – he was indignant; ἐντεῦθεν – at that moment.

74   τὸν πάντα λόγον – the whole story (*NB this meaning of* πάντα *when it is in between the article and noun; in the predicative position, where it is mostly found, it means 'every'*); ἐξαπατηθείς – (*participle after* ὡς = on the grounds that) he had been cheated; διδόασιν – 3rd plur. present indicative active of δίδωμι (*NB the use of the historic present here*).

75   εἵλετο – *see l.65*; αὐτίκα – straightaway; ἔμφυτος -ον – inborn, naturally-inspired (*fem. acc. sing: the compound adj. only has two terminations*); μαντικός -ή -όν (< mantic) – prophetic (*the two adjectives are agreeing with an understood noun* τέχνην = skill, power); *translate the phrase as* 'a naturally inspired prophetic power' (*i.e. Euenius spontaneously gained this gift, rather than having to learn it over years of study of signs and portents etc.*).

76   ὀνομαστός -ή -όν (> ὄνομα) – renowned.

> Q. Do you think that Euenius was justified in feeling so indignant? Lay out arguments for and against his response.
>
> Q. Consider the gods' reference, in their oracular responses, to this last gift that Euenius will receive: why would it be considered such a source of envy?
>
> Q. Suggest a reason why Herodotus does not mention whether the Apollonians were rid of the blight on their produce and flocks.

Respect for suppliants enforced by an oracle

The people of Cyme are uncertain how to deal with a man taking refuge from the Persians with them and ask advice from the oracle. The response of the god divides opinion.

ὁ μὲν Πακτύης, δείσας τοὺς Πέρσας, ᾤχετο φεύγων
εἰς Κύμην· ὁ δὲ Μαζάρης ἔπεμπεν εἰς τὴν Κύμην
ἀγγέλους, ἐκδιδόναι κελεύων Πακτύην. οἱ δὲ Κυμαῖοι
ἔγνωσαν συμβουλῆς πέρι εἰς θεὸν τὸν ἐν Βραγχίδαις   80
ἀναφέρειν. ἦν γὰρ αὐτόθι μαντεῖον ἐκ παλαιοῦ ἱδρυμένον,
ᾧ Ἴωνές τε πάντες καὶ Αἰολεῖς εἰώθεσαν χρῆσθαι.
πέμψαντες οὖν οἱ Κυμαῖοι θεοπρόπους ἠρώτων ὁποῖόν
τι περὶ Πακτύην ποιοῦντες θεοῖς μέλλοιεν χαριεῖσθαι.
ἐπερωτῶσι δὲ αὐτοῖς ταῦτα χρηστήριον ἐγένετο   85
ἐκδιδόναι Πακτύην τοῖς Πέρσαις.
ταῦτα δὲ ὡς ἤκουσαν οἱ Κυμαῖοι ὡρμῶντο ἐκδιδόναι·
ὁρμωμένου δὲ τοῦ πλήθους, Ἀριστόδικος, ἀνὴρ τῶν
ἀστῶν δόκιμος, ἔσχε μὴ ποιῆσαι ταῦτα τοὺς Κυμαίους,
ἀπιστῶν τε τῷ χρησμῷ, καὶ δοκῶν τοὺς θεοπρόπους οὐ   90
λέγειν ἀληθῶς· εἰς ὅ, τὸ δεύτερον περὶ Πακτύου ἐπερησόμενοι,
ἦσαν ἄλλοι θεοπρόποι ὧν καὶ Ἀριστόδικος ἦν.

Names and places

Πακτύης -ου ὁ: Pactyes, *a Lydian (from Lydia, modern south-west Turkey): in c. 546 BCE, after his defeat of the Lydian king, Cyrus, the Persian King, made Pactyes responsible for collecting the tribute from Lydia. But, instead, he induced the Lydians to revolt and went on the run when Cyrus sent an army in response.*

Πέρσαι -ῶν οἱ: The Persians. *A collective name given to the ethnic groups living in the vast empire of the Persian King.*

Κύμη -ης ἡ: Cyme, *a Greek city on the Ionian coast (western Turkey). Ionian Greece was the interface between the world of Greece and that of Persia. The relationship between the Greek cities and the Persians veered between self-governing independence and tribute-paying vassalage under the Persian King. The King's representatives, called Satraps, oversaw his interest in the region.*

Κυμαῖοι -ων οἱ: The Cymaeans, *the people of Cyme.*

Μαζάρης -ου ὁ: Mazares, *one of King Cyrus' generals.*

Βραγχίδαι -ῶν αἱ: Branchidae, *originally called Didyma, was the site of the oracle of Apollo, the most important oracle for the Ionian Greeks, near Miletus.*

Ἴωνες -ων οἱ: The Ionians, *a major ethnic division of the Greek people who had founded 12 cities in the southern part of the modern-day west coast of Turkey.*

Αἰολεῖς -έων οἱ: The Aeolians, *another ethnic division of the Greeks who had migrated mostly to the modern-day western coast of Turkey to the north of the Ionians.*

Ἀριστόδικος -ου ὁ: Aristodicus, *an inhabitant of Cyme.*

> **GCSE vocabulary:** ἄγγελος, ἀκούω, ἀληθής, ἄλλος, ἀνήρ, αὐτόν, γάρ, γίγνομαι, γιγνώσκω, δέ, δίδωμι (ἐκδιδόναι), εἰς (ἐς), εἰμί, εἶμι, ἐκ, ἐρωτάω, ἔχω, θεός, καί, κελεύω, λέγω, μέν… δέ…, μέλλω, μή, ὅς, οὐ, οὖν, οὗτος, πᾶς, πέμπω, περί, ποιέω, ποῖος (ὁποῖος), τε… καί…, φεύγω, χράομαι, ὡς.

77 δείσας (*aorist participle act of* δείδω) – in fear of; οἴχομαι – be gone, go.
79 ἐκδιδόναι (*present infinitive of* ἐκδίδωμι) – to hand over.
80 γιγνώσκω – (*here*) decide (+ *infinitive*); συμβουλή -ῆς ἡ – advice; πέρι + *gen.* – for (*the preposition here is placed after the noun it governs*).
81 ἐς… ἀναφέρειν – to go to consult; αὐτόθι – there; μαντεῖον -ου τό – oracle; ἐκ παλαιοῦ (< palaeontology) (> πάλαι) – (*adverbial phrase*) from antiquity; ἱδρυμένος -η -ον – established.
82 εἰώθεσαν (*3rd plur. pluperfect from* εἴωθα) – were accustomed; χράομαι + *dat.* – consult (*here*).
83 θεοπρόπος -ου ὁ – oracular legate (*sent to consult an oracle*); ὁποῖος -α -ον (*equivalent of* ποῖος *used in an indirect question; taken with* τι (l.84) *it forms the object of* ποιοῦντες *also in l.84*) – what sort of (thing).
84 μέλλοιεν – *present optative, replacing indicative in an indirect question in historic sequence*; χαριεῖσθαι (*future infinitive of* χαρίζομαι) + *dat.* – to please.
85 ἐπερωτῶσι (*masc. dat. plur. of the present participle of* ἐπερωτάω; *agreeing with* αὐτοῖς) – asking; χρηστήριον -ου τό (> χράομαι) – oracle; γίγνομαι – am made, am given (*see l. 72*).
86 ἐκδιδόναι – *see l.79* (*the infinitive expresses an indirect command implied by* χρηστήριον).
87 ὁρμάομαι – be eager (to) (+ *infinitive*).
88 πλῆθος -ους τό (> plethora) – the majority.
89 ἀστός – citizen; δόκιμος – notable; ἔχω (*here* + *acc.* + μή + *infinitive*) – restrain X (from doing Y).
90 ἀπιστέω (> πιστεύω) – disbelieve (+ *dat.*); χρησμός -οῦ ὁ – oracular response; δοκέω – think (*NB distinguish this personal use of the verb from the impersonal form,* δοκεῖ); θεοπρόπος – *see l.83*.
91 εἰς ὅ – in response to this; τὸ δεύτερον (< deuterium) – (*adverbial*) for the second time; ἐπερησόμενοι (*from* ἐπερωτάω, *see l.85; here the future participle indicates purpose*) – to put a question.
92 ᾖσαν – *3rd plur. past tense of* εἶμι (go).

> Q. What do you think made the presence of Pactyes in Cyme a problem?
> Q. Why does Herodotus stress the importance of the oracle at Branchidae?
> Q. Where does Aristodicus suggest the problem of interpreting the god's words may lie?

Aristodicus enquires of the oracle again and is given the same response as the first set of Cymaean messengers; he therefore tries to prove a point to the god of the oracle.

ἀφικομένων δὲ αὐτῶν εἰς Βραγχίδας, ἐχρηστηριάζετο
ἐκ πάντων Ἀριστόδικος ἐπερωτῶν τάδε, "ὦναξ, ἦλθε
παρ' ἡμᾶς ἱκέτης Πακτύης ὁ Λυδός, φεύγων θάνατον   95
βίαιον πρὸς Περσῶν· οἱ δὲ αὐτὸν ἐξαιτοῦνται προεῖναι
Κυμαίους κελεύοντες. ἡμεῖς δέ, δειμαίνοντες τὴν Περσῶν
δύναμιν, τὸν ἱκέτην εἰς τόδε οὐ τετολμήκαμεν ἐκδιδόναι
πρὶν ἂν τὸ ἀπὸ σοῦ ἡμῖν δηλωθῇ ἀκριβῶς ὁπότερα
ποιῶμεν."   100
ὁ μὲν ταῦτα ἐπηρώτα· ὁ δὲ θεὸς αὖθις τὸν αὐτὸν
χρησμὸν ἔφαινε, κελεύων ἐκδιδόναι Πακτύην τοῖς Πέρσαις.
πρὸς ταῦτα ὁ Ἀριστόδικος ἐκ προνοίας ἐποίει τάδε·
περιὼν τὸν νεὼν κύκλῳ ἐξῄρει τοὺς στρουθούς, καὶ
ἄλλα ὅσα ἦν νενεοττευμένα ὀρνίθων γένη ἐν τῷ νεῴ.   105

Name
Λυδός -οῦ ὁ: Lydian, *someone from Lydia*.

Supplication
Supplication – the action carried out by a suppliant – was a way of making a request more compelling. A supplication can be made to a person or, most commonly, to a god: the object is firstly to acknowledge the greater power or authority of the person being supplicated, and secondly to make a humble request of that person in the light of their superiority. Supplication of a mortal becomes more powerful if physical contact with the person being supplicated is made, conventionally, on the knees in front of the person, grasping their knees with one arm and reaching up to their beard with the other hand: this posture of humility and vulnerability shows that the suppliant is unarmed and can be killed easily if the other wished to. A god is supplicated by prayer or, as here, by approaching an intermediary such as an oracle; however, Aristodicus appears to neglect the humility which must always be the central element of the process of supplication.

> Q. How does Aristodicus' personal question to the oracle at Branchidae differ from the original? Why do you think that Aristodicus has made these adjustments?
>
> Q. How does the last comment of Aristodicus, lines 99–100, reveal that he sees the essence of the problem as one of miscommunication?
>
> Q. Before turning over the page, try to anticipate the point that Aristodicus' action in clearing away the birds in the temple is designed to make.

GCSE vocabulary: ἀφικνέομαι, αἰτέω, ἄλλος, ἀπό, αὖθις, αὐτός, δέ, δίδωμι (ἐκδιδόναι), εἰς (ἐς), εἰμί, εἶμι, ἐκ, ἐν, ἔρχομαι, ἐρωτάω, ἡμεῖς, θάνατος, θεός, καί, κελεύω, μέν … δέ … , ὅδε, οὐ, οὗτος, πᾶς, παρά, ποιέω, πόσος (ὅσος), πρός, σύ, φεύγω.

93 χρηστηριάζομαι – consult an oracle.
94 ἐκ πάντων – (lit. *out of them all*) on behalf of them all; ἐπερωτάω – see *l.85*; ὦναξ = ὦ ἄναξ (crasis, *see p.81*) – O lord.
95 ἱκέτης -ου ὁ – a suppliant (*someone who puts themselves at the mercy of another*).
96 βίαιος -α -ον – violent; πρός + gen. – at the hands of; αὐτόν – *object of both* ἐξαιτοῦνται *and* προεῖναι; ἐξαιτέομαι (> αἰτέω) – demand; προεῖναι (*aor infin act*) – to surrender (*transitive*).
97 δειμαίνω – fear (*the participle here has concessive force: 'although...'*).
98 δύναμις -εως ἡ – power; εἰς τόδε – until now; τετολμήκαμεν (*1st plural perfect active of* τολμάω) – we have dared; ἐκδιδόναι – to hand over (*see l.79*).
99 πρὶν ἄν (+ *subjunctive, the indefinite construction*) – until such time as; τὸ ἀπὸ σοῦ – your response (*lit. = the thing from you*); δηλόω (δηλωθῇ *is aorist subjunctive passive, part of the indefinite construction introduced by* πρίν) – reveal; ἀκριβῶς – accurately; ὁπότερα (*lit – which of the two things, neut. acc. plur., introducing an indirect question*) – which action (*i.e. to surrender Pactyes or to protect him*).
100 ποιῶμεν (*present subjunctive indicating that the question here reported is a deliberative one*) – we are to take.
102 χρησμόν – oracular response (*see l. 90*); φαίνω (> φαίνομαι) (< phenomenon) – reveal; ἐκδιδόναι – *see l.98*.
103 πρός + acc. – in response to (*see l.73*); ἐκ προνοίας – deliberately.
104 περιιών (> εἶμι) – going around; νεώς νεώ ὁ – temple; κύκλος -ου ὁ (< cycle) – circle; ἐξαιρέω – remove (*the imperfect tense indicates that he 'began to' do this*); στρουθός -οῦ ὁ – sparrow.
105 ἄλλα – *neut. plur. agreeing with* γένη; *the adjective is placed outside the relative clause in which it belongs*; ὅσοι -αι -α (> πόσος) – as many ... as (*agreeing with* γένη); ἦν νενεοττευμένα – had been hatched; ὄρνις -ιθος ὁ/ἡ (< ornithology) – bird; γένος -ους τό (< genealogy) – type.

Figure 3 *Temple of Apollo at Didyma: the site of the Oracle of Branchidae consulted by Aristodicus and his fellow citizens of Cyme to resolve their dilemma over what to do with Pactyes, a fugitive from the Persians.*
Photo: Getty (cemagraphics).

The god responds angrily to Aristodicus' actions and gives a surprising explanation for his instructions.

ποιοῦντος δὲ αὐτοῦ ταῦτα, φωνὴ ἐκ τοῦ ἀδύτου ἐγένετο
λέγουσα τάδε, "ἀνοσιώτατε ἀνθρώπων, τί τάδε τολμᾷς
ποιεῖν; τοὺς ἱκέτας μου ἐκ τοῦ νεὼ κεραΐζεις;" Ἀριστόδικος
δὲ οὐκ ἀπορήσας πρὸς ταῦτα εἶπεν, "ὦναξ, αὐτὸς
μὲν οὕτω τοῖς ἱκέταις βοηθεῖς, Κυμαίους δὲ κελεύεις τὸν   110
ἱκέτην ἐκδιδόναι." ὁ δὲ θεὸς αὖθις ἠμείψατο τοῖσδε,
"ναὶ κελεύω, ἵνα γε ἀσεβήσαντες θᾶττον ἀπόλησθε,
ὡς μὴ τὸ λοιπὸν περὶ ἱκετῶν ἐκδόσεως ἔλθητε ἐπὶ τὸ
χρηστήριον."

Herodotus' use of direct (& indirect) speech

It strikes us as strange that a writer of history should include in their account so much speech, both direct (as in this story and that of Euenius) and indirect (as in the story of Arion). It is clear that Herodotus himself could not have been present at the encounters which he describes, just as it is unlikely that there existed any formal record of what was said which he could have drawn upon. Of course, such fabrication provided fuel to the claims of some ancient commentators that Herodotus was not so much the 'Father of History' as the 'Father of Lies'. However, in Herodotus' heavy use of imagined speech in the 'Histories', it is more useful to recognise his debt to the epic poems of Homer, not only because he understood them to be the epitome of narrative of the past, but also because, in them, speech plays a critical role in presenting motive for actions and reaction to them: elements which are both central to any account of 'the past'. Secondly, Herodotus is very conscious of the dramatic impact which speech helps to generate in narrative and he is a consummate storyteller who wishes to engage his reader in the wonder of the events he describes. Finally, to someone who lived in a world in which the transmission of ideas and information was primarily conducted orally, the representation of that oral way of life through imagined speech would be considered to enliven a narrative, thus making it more realistic rather than detracting in any way from its credibility.

> Q. What is different about the god's response in lines 107–8 from any previous response?
>
> Q. Do you think that Aristodicus' actions are clever or foolhardy? Explain your reasoning.
>
> Q. In line 112, the god describes the Cymaeans altogether (not just Aristodicus) as impious – what has been impious about their actions?
>
> Q. What is perhaps in the god's mind when he speaks of their imminent destruction?
>
> Q. Explain how this story, as its title suggests, reinforces respect for suppliants.

> **GCSE vocabulary:** αὖθις, ἄνθρωπος, αὐτόν, βοηθέω, γε, γίγνομαι, δέ, δίδωμι (ἐκδιδόναι), ἐγώ, ἐκ, ἐπί, ἔρχομαι, θεός, ἵνα, κελεύω, λέγω, μέν… δέ…, μή, ὅδε, οὐ, οὗτος, οὕτω, περί, ποιέω, πρός, ταχύς (θᾶσσον), τί, φωνή, ὡς.

106 ἄδυτον -ου τό – inner sanctuary.
107 ἀνόσιος -ον – impious; τί – why?; τολμάω – dare (see l.98).
108 ἱκέτης – a suppliant (see l.95); νεώς – temple (see l.104); κεραΐζω – uproot.
109 ἀπορέω – be disconcerted; ὦναξ – O lord (see l.94).
111 ἐκδιδόναι – to hand over (see l.79); ἀμείβομαι (aorist ἠμειψάμην) – respond.
112 ναί - yes, indeed (emphatic affirmative); ἀσεβέω – be impious; θᾶττον (comparative adverb of ταχύς) – more quickly; ἀπόλησθε (2nd plur. aorist subjunctive middle of ἀπόλλυμι: subjunctive in purpose clause introduced by ἵνα) – you may be destroyed.
113 ὡς = ἵνα (+ subjunctive, introducing a second purpose clause); τὸ λοιπόν – in the future (see l.68); ἐκδόσις -εως ἡ (> ἐκδιδόναι) – surrender.
114 χρηστήριον -ου τό (> χρησμός) – oracular shrine (contrast this meaning with that in l.85 to refer to the response issued by the oracle: there is often little distinction between the oracle that is given and the place from which it is given).

What happens next?

The people of Cyme continue to be conflicted by the problem presented by Pactyes. First, they despatch him to Mytilene on the island of Lesbos, but when the Mytilenians are about to hand him over to the Persians, the people of Cyme intervene and take him off to the island of Chios. The Chians, however, forcibly remove Pactyes from the temple of Apollo where he was taking sanctuary and hand him to the Persians in exchange for some land on the mainland.

Final questions

- Which scenes stand out most vividly from this selection?
- What are Herodotus' strengths as a writer?
- What insight do these extracts give into the moral tone of Herodotus' work?
- Does Herodotus appear to show any sympathy for the difficulty that mortals have in their capacity to communicate with the divine?
- Is there a place for anecdotes of this sort in serious 'history'?

Lysias

Lysias was one of the most admired orators of ancient Athens, but he was not actually an Athenian. Rather he was a metic, or resident alien, in Athens, the son of a rich Syracusan called Cephalos, who had also lived in the city and been a friend of several Athenian aristocrats. Metics did not enjoy the political rights of the citizens and had to pay a special metic tax, but despite this, lots of people chose to live in Athens as metics because of the economic appeal of the city. Indeed, Lysias, together with his brother, Polemarchus, owned a shield factory and they were rich enough to be selected for execution by the Thirty Tyrants, the ruling junta that was set up by the Spartans in Athens at the end of the Peloponnesian War in 404 BCE: his brother was killed, Lysias narrowly escaped, and a great deal of the family's property was confiscated to finance the regime.

It is not certain how Lysias developed his rhetorical skill, but it is said that he studied rhetoric when he joined the panhellenic colony of Thurii in southern Italy. However, there is no evidence of his involvement in oratory after his return to Athens in 412 BCE, until after his attempt to seek legal redress for the murder of his brother once the democracy was restored in Athens. He prosecuted Eratosthenes, one of the Thirty (not the man of the same name who was the victim of the case in the set text), and the speech that he delivered on that occasion survives in the extant corpus of Lysias' orations (as number 12). It seems likely that it was this event and the publicity it achieved that led him to develop his career as a teacher of rhetoric and as a speech-writer (or logographer).

Indeed, the rest of the speeches of Lysias which survive were written not for delivery by Lysias himself, but by others who came to him and paid him to produce a speech for them to deliver in court as if it were their own handiwork. In normal circumstances the courts in Athens, unlike those of modern Britain (or indeed of Rome), required the litigants to make their own case in person, rather than hire specialist lawyers to make the case on their behalf. For those who were politically engaged and expert orators, this would not have presented a challenge but, from the last quarter of the fifth century BCE, it became possible for those who needed help to approach a logographer who would compose a speech for them. Presumably there was a consultation process, during which the logographer would not only find out the details of the case, but also the character of his client, so that he could compose something appropriate; the fiction had to be maintained that the speech was the work of the plaintiff himself. The Athenians strongly disapproved of the idea of writing speeches for pay and disliked the idea that anyone should be able to purchase a better speech by means of his wealth, which would render the chances in the case unequal. As a result, the logographer had to remain anonymous: this anonymity also means that it is hard to be certain that all of the speeches which survive under his name are genuinely by Lysias, but there is little doubt in the case of the speech which is the current set text.

2025–26 Prescription

This selection corresponds to Lysias 1. 6–27, with the omission of a small part from sections 15–16. The text used is that printed in J. Taylor, *Greek Beyond GCSE* pp. 250–6.

We know nothing of the circumstances of the case beyond what we learn from the speech itself, which is of course problematic, since we only have one perspective on events. Euphiletos, the defendant, is being prosecuted for the murder of a man called Eratosthenes, a killing which seems beyond dispute, and which happened in his own house. His defence is that Eratosthenes was conducting an adulterous affair with Euphiletos' wife, and therefore his killing was justified by the Athenian law on adultery, which allowed the killing of any man that one caught in the act with one's wife (or indeed with any woman under a man's control, including a free mistress). Besides the perspective the speech offers on attitudes towards adultery in ancient Athens, it also gives a rich picture of Athenian domestic life, but it is important always to remember the context of the text to avoid drawing excessively simplistic conclusions from it about Athenian practices and attitudes.

Cases were heard in a single day before large juries presided over by one of the annual magistrates. As in a modern trial, the prosecution spoke before the defence (a set amount of time was allocated to the speakers by the use of a water-clock), but, as we have seen, the plaintiffs were expected to speak in person. In this case the prosecution would have been conducted by male relatives of the dead Eratosthenes. The jury was usually made up of several hundred citizens, drawn by lot on the day of the trial to limit the possibility of bribery. The jurors were supposed to be representative of the citizen body as a whole, although it is likely that the urban poor were somewhat overrepresented. Lysias, therefore, could only make Euphiletos express opinions and display attitudes which he thought would appeal to the majority of these men, which suggests that the text would be a rich repository of widely held thoughts and ideas. However, everything that is included in the speech (and just as importantly omitted from it) will ultimately reflect what Lysias thought was most conducive to Euphiletos winning his case.

The speech so far

The extract you will read is almost the entirety of Lysias' account of the events that are at issue in the case (the *narratio*, or *diegesis* in Greek). The speech had opened with a slightly more rhetorical passage in which Lysias sought to win over the jury to sympathise with Euphiletos. He did so by asking them to imagine that the adultery had been committed against them, and drawing attention to the seriousness of adultery by arguing that all Greek states viewed it with equal gravity, whatever the relative social status of the victim and the perpetrator. He then sets out simply what he plans to show to the court, including the fact that he had no prior grudge against Eratosthenes, or indeed any other motive for killing him. He promises to leave nothing out, but to tell the whole truth.

Euphiletos describes the start of his marriage in positive terms, until the death of his mother, which signals the beginning of his marital problems (Lysias 1. 6–8).

ἐγὼ γάρ, ὦ Ἀθηναῖοι, ἐπειδὴ ἔδοξέ μοι γῆμαι καὶ γυναῖκα
ἠγαγόμην εἰς τὴν οἰκίαν, τὸν μὲν ἄλλον χρόνον οὕτω διεκείμην
ὥστε μήτε λυπεῖν μήτε λίαν ἐπ' ἐκείνῃ εἶναι ὅ τι ἂν ἐθέλῃ
ποιεῖν, ἐφύλαττόν τε ὡς οἷόν τε ἦν, καὶ προσεῖχον τὸν νοῦν
ὥσπερ εἰκὸς ἦν· ἐπειδὴ δέ μοι παιδίον γίγνεται, ἐπίστευον ἤδη   5
καὶ πάντα τὰ ἐμαυτοῦ ἐκείνῃ παρέδωκα, ἡγούμενος ταύτην
οἰκειότητα μεγίστην εἶναι· ἐν μὲν οὖν τῷ πρώτῳ χρόνῳ, ὦ
Ἀθηναῖοι, πασῶν ἦν βελτίστη· καὶ γὰρ οἰκονόμος δεινὴ καὶ
φειδωλὸς καὶ ἀκριβῶς πάντα διοικοῦσα· ἐπειδὴ δέ μοι ἡ μήτηρ
ἐτελεύτησεν, πάντων τῶν κακῶν ἀποθανοῦσα αἰτία μοι   10
γεγένηται· ἐπ' ἐκφορὰν γὰρ αὐτῇ ἀκολουθήσασα ἡ ἐμὴ γυνὴ
ὑπὸ τούτου τοῦ ἀνθρώπου ὀφθεῖσα, χρόνῳ διαφθείρεται·
ἐπιτηρῶν γὰρ τὴν θεράπαιναν τὴν εἰς τὴν ἀγορὰν βαδίζουσαν
καὶ λόγους προσφέρων ἀπώλεσεν αὐτήν.

Athenian weddings

In a wedding, there was a banquet at the house of the bride's father and then, in the evening, the groom took the bride to his house in a procession. Here she was received into her new husband's house by the same rite with which new slaves were received into the house. Then the marriage was consummated in the bridal chamber while friends sang a wedding song outside. Therefore, the marriage ceremony symbolised a woman's transfer from the control of her father to that of her husband and reinforced the fact that the production of children was the prime function of marriage.

Athenian funerals

After a death, the corpse was formally laid out in the house and prepared for the funeral by female relatives. The lead role in the lament was taken by these women: they would dress in black with their hair shorn, and would beat their breasts while singing. The women would also participate in the funeral procession when the body would be wrapped in a shroud and conducted to the burial ground (the ἐκφορά, see line 11) to be buried or cremated. This procession was therefore potentially one of the few occasions when higher-status women could be seen by other men outside the house, and beyond the direct control and supervision of their husbands.

> Q. How do you think that Lysias is trying to present Euphiletos' behaviour as a new husband?
>
> Q. Why do you think that the birth of a child changes the relationship between Euphiletos and his wife?
>
> Q. What qualities does Lysias make Euphiletos praise in his wife?
>
> Q. What does it say about Athenian attitudes to marriage that Euphiletos is made to use the verb διαφθείρεται of his wife as a result of the affair?

GCSE vocabulary: ἀγορά, ἄγω, Ἀθηναῖοι, αἴτιος, ἄλλος, ἄνθρωπος, ἀποθνῄσκω, αὐτός, γάρ, γίγνομαι, γυνή, δεινός, διαφθείρω, δοκεῖ, ἐγώ, ἐθέλω, εἰμί, εἰς, ἐκεῖνος, ἐμός, ἐν, ἐπί, ἤδη, καί, κακός, λόγος, μέγας, μέν… δέ…, μήτε… μήτε…, μήτηρ, μοι, οἰκία, οἷός τ' εἰμί, ὁράω (ὤφθην), οὖν, οὗτος, οὕτω, πᾶς, πιστεύω, ποιέω, πρῶτος, ὑπό, φυλάττω, χρόνος, ὦ, ὡς, ὥστε.

1 ὦ Ἀθηναῖοι – *this form of vocative address is often used by speakers towards juries in the Athenian courts*; ἐπειδή = ἐπεί; γαμέω (< bigamy) – *(aorist* ἔγημα*)* marry.
2 ἄγομαι – *in the middle voice ('I take for myself') this verb is often used of a man bringing home a bride*; τὸν μὲν ἄλλον χρόνον – *translate as* 'for some time', *contrasting with* ἐπειδὴ δέ *in l.5*; διεκείμην *(imperfect of* διάκειμαι*)* – 'I was disposed'.
3 λυπέω – annoy, upset; λίαν – excessively; ἐπ' ἐκείνῃ εἶναι – '(for it) to be in her power' *(followed by the infinitive* ποιεῖν*)*; ὅ τι ἄν – *introducing an indefinite construction with the subjunctive* (ἐθέλῃ): 'whatever she wanted'.
4 φυλάττω – keep watch (*here*); τε – and (*linking this clause to the previous one, coming as usual second in its clause*); ὡς οἷόν τε ἦν – 'as far as possible'; προσέχω τὸν νοῦν – pay attention.
5 ὥσπερ (> ὡς) – just as; εἰκός -ότος τό – (what is) reasonable; ἐπειδή – *see l.1*; παιδίον τό (*diminutive >* παῖς) – baby; γίγνεται – *historic present: translate as past*.
6 ἐμαυτόν – myself: τὰ ἐμαυτοῦ – 'my own affairs'; παραδίδωμι (> δίδωμι) – hand over; ἡγέομαι – think, consider.
7 οἰκειότης -ητος ἡ – intimacy; ὁ πρῶτος χρόνος – 'the first period'.
8 βέλτιστος -η -ον = ἄριστος; καὶ γάρ – for in fact: *supply* 'she was' (ἦν); οἰκονόμος ὁ/ἡ (> οἰκία & νόμος) – housekeeper; δεινός -ή -όν – clever (*here*).
9 φειδωλός -όν – thrifty (*a two-termination adjective with no separate feminine form*); ἀκριβῶς – exactly, precisely; διοικέω (> οἰκέω) – organise; ἐπειδή – *see l.1*; μοι – *dative of disadvantage: here translate as* 'my'.
10 τελευτάω (> τέλος) – die.
11 γεγένηται – (*perfect of* γίγνομαι) 'has become'; ἐκφορά ἡ (> ἐκ & φέρω) – funeral; αὐτῇ – *refers to the speaker's dead mother*; ἀκολουθέω + dat. – follow.
12 χρόνῳ - in time; διαφθείρεται – *historic present (see l.5)*.
13 ἐπιτηρέω – keep watch for; θεράπαινα ἡ (< therapy) – slave-woman; βαδίζω – walk, go.
14 προσφέρω (> φέρω) – offer, use; ἀπόλλυμι (aorist ἀπώλεσα) – corrupt; αὐτήν – *refers to the slave-woman*.

Euphiletos explains how after the birth of a child the domestic arrangements were altered. However, this change is exploited by his wife (Lysias 1. 9–11).

πρῶτον μὲν οὖν, ὦ ἄνδρες, (δεῖ γὰρ καὶ ταῦθ᾽ ὑμῖν   15
διηγήσασθαι) οἰκίδιον ἔστι μοι διπλοῦν, ἴσα ἔχον τὰ ἄνω τοῖς
κάτω κατὰ τὴν γυναικωνῖτιν καὶ κατὰ τὴν ἀνδρωνῖτιν. ἐπειδὴ
δὲ τὸ παιδίον ἐγένετο ἡμῖν, ἡ μήτηρ αὐτὸ ἐθήλαζεν· ἵνα δὲ μή,
ὁπότε λοῦσθαι δέοι, κινδυνεύῃ κατὰ τῆς κλίμακος
καταβαίνουσα, ἐγὼ μὲν ἄνω διῃτώμην, αἱ δὲ γυναῖκες κάτω.   20
καὶ οὕτως ἤδη συνειθισμένον ἦν, ὥστε πολλάκις ἡ γυνὴ ἀπῄει
κάτω καθευδήσουσα ὡς τὸ παιδίον, ἵνα τὸν τιτθὸν αὐτῷ διδῷ
καὶ μὴ βοᾷ. καὶ ταῦτα πολὺν χρόνον οὕτως ἐγίγνετο, καὶ ἐγὼ
οὐδέποτε ὑπώπτευσα, ἀλλ᾽ οὕτως ἠλιθίως διεκείμην, ὥστε
ᾤμην τὴν ἐμαυτοῦ γυναῖκα πασῶν σωφρονεστάτην εἶναι τῶν   25
ἐν τῇ πόλει.

προϊόντος δὲ τοῦ χρόνου, ὦ ἄνδρες, ἧκον μὲν ἀπροσδοκήτως ἐξ
ἀγροῦ, μετὰ δὲ τὸ δεῖπνον τὸ παιδίον ἐβόα καὶ ἐδυσκόλαινεν
ὑπὸ τῆς θεραπαίνης ἐπίτηδες λυπούμενον, ἵνα ταῦτα ποιῇ· ὁ
γὰρ ἄνθρωπος ἔνδον ἦν· ὕστερον γὰρ ἅπαντα ἐπυθόμην.   30

Athenian domestic lives

Women in Athens lived very different lives from their husbands even within the home. Near the entrance to the house would be the main room for men (*andron*), the location for holding *symposia*, male drinking parties, which would not normally be attended by the free women of the household. The women's quarters would be away from the entrance, whether at the back of the house or, as in this case, upstairs. Here the women of the house, supervised by the wife of the head of the household, would be involved in domestic activities, the most notable of which would have been the weaving of cloth on a loom. The exact role played by the wife would depend on social circumstances. In this case, she does not appear to use a wet nurse, but breastfeeds the baby herself, even though the family is rich enough to have a slave woman to shop in the agora (see lines 13–14 above), whom Eratosthenes has to approach as a go-between in order to make further contact with Euphiletos' wife. Moreover, the family has enough wealth to own some land in the country (lines 27–8).

Q. Why do you think Lysias makes Euphiletos refer to his house with a diminutive (οἰκίδιον)?

Q. Why is there so much detail about Euphiletos' domestic arrangements here?

Q. What impression of Euphiletos does Lysias seek to present to the jurors in this passage?

Q. What effect does it have that Eratosthenes is not named here, but just referred to as ὁ ἄνθρωπος?

GCSE vocabulary: *ἀγρός, ἀλλά, ἀνήρ, ἄνθρωπος, αὐτός, βαίνω (καταβαίνω), βοάω, γάρ, γίγνομαι, γυνή, δεῖ, δεῖπνον, ἐγώ, εἰμί, εἶμι (ἄπειμι), ἐν, ἐξ, ἔχω, ἤδη, ἡμεῖς, ἵνα, καθεύδω, καί, κατά, μέν… δέ…, μετά (+ acc.), μή, μήτηρ, οὐδέποτε, οὖν, οὗτος, οὕτως, πᾶς, ποιέω, πόλις, πολλάκις, πολύς, πρῶτον, πυνθάνομαι, ὑμεῖς, ὑπό, ὕστερον, χρόνος, ὦ, ὥστε.*

15 **καί** – also; **ταῦθ'** = ταῦτα (*elision with aspiration consequent on the next word beginning with a rough breathing*).
16 **διηγέομαι** (< diegesis) – explain, give an account of; **οἰκίδιον τό** (> οἰκία) – little house (*a diminutive*); **ἔστι μοι** – (*possessive dative*) 'I have'; **διπλοῦς -ῆ -οῦν** (< diploma) – two-storey; **ἴσος -η -ον** (< isosceles) – equal; **τὰ ἄνω** (> ἀνά) – the upstairs.
17 **τὰ κάτω** (> κατά) – the downstairs; **κατά + acc.** – for (*here*); **γυναικωνῖτις -ιδος ἡ** (> γυνή) – women's quarters; **ἀνδρωνῖτις -ιδος ἡ** (> ἀνήρ) – men's quarters; **ἐπειδή** – when (*see l.1*).
18 **παιδίον** – *see l.5*; **θηλάζω** – suckle, breastfeed.
19 **ὁπότε** – when(ever); **λοῦσθαι** = λούεσθαι, *passive infinitive of* λούω – wash; **δέοι** – *the optative of* δεῖ *is used here in the indefinite construction: translate as* 'whenever it needed …'; **κινδυνεύω** (> κίνδυνος) – be in danger; **κλῖμαξ -ακος ἡ** (< climax) – ladder, staircase.
20 **ἄνω** – *see l.16*; **διαιτάομαι** – live; **κάτω** – *see l.17*.
21 **συνειθισμένον ἦν** – (*impersonal pluperfect passive of* συνεθίζω) 'it had become customary'; **ἀπῄει** (*3rd sing. imperfect of* ἄπειμι) – go away.
22 **καθευδήσουσα** – *future participle to express purpose*; **ὡς + acc.** – to; **τιτθός ὁ** – breast; **διδῷ** (*3rd sing. present subjunctive of* δίδωμι) – give, offer.
23 **βοᾷ** (*3rd sing. pres. subj. of* βοάω) – cry (*note the unstated change of subject*).
24 **ὑποπτεύω** – suspect; **ἠλιθίως** – foolishly; **διεκείμην** – 'I was disposed' (*see l.2*).
25 **ᾤμην** (*imperfect of* οἴμαι) – 'I thought'; **ἐμαυτόν** – myself; **πασῶν** – *agrees with* τῶν ἐν τῇ πόλει; **σώφρων -ονος** – of good sense, faithful.
27 **πρόειμι** (> πρό & εἶμι) – elapse, pass; **ἧκον** – *imperfect, with pluperfect meaning, of* ἥκω, I have come, have returned; **ἀπροσδοκήτως** (> δέχομαι) – unexpectedly.
28 **ἀγρός ὁ** – country, countryside (*here*); **δυσκολαίνω** – be unhappy.
29 **θεραπαίνα** – slave-woman (*see l.13*); **ἐπίτηδες** – deliberately; **λυπέω** – annoy, upset (*see l.3*).
30 **ἔνδον** (> ἐν) – inside, in the house; **ἅπαντα** – (*from a strengthened form of* πᾶς) 'absolutely everything'.

After his wife initially feigns reluctance to go to feed the baby, there are subsequently various suspicious goings-on in the night. Euphiletos does not follow up his suspicions the next morning (Lysias 1. 12–14).

καὶ ἐγὼ τὴν γυναῖκα ἀπιέναι ἐκέλευον καὶ δοῦναι τῷ παιδίῳ
τὸν τιτθόν, ἵνα παύσηται κλᾶον. ἡ δὲ τὸ μὲν πρῶτον οὐκ
ἤθελεν, ὡς ἂν ἀσμένη με ἑωρακυῖα ἥκοντα διὰ χρόνου· ἐπειδὴ
δὲ ἐγὼ ὠργιζόμην καὶ ἐκέλευον αὐτὴν ἀπιέναι, "ἵνα σύ γε,"
ἔφη, "πειρᾷς ἐνταῦθα τὴν παιδίσκην· καὶ πρότερον δὲ μεθύων   35
εἷλκες αὐτήν." κἀγὼ μὲν ἐγέλων, ἐκείνη δὲ ἀναστᾶσα καὶ
ἀπιοῦσα προστίθησι τὴν θύραν, προσποιουμένη παίζειν, καὶ
τὴν κλεῖν ἐφέλκεται. κἀγὼ τούτων οὐδὲν ἐνθυμούμενος οὐδ᾽
ὑπονοῶν ἐκάθευδον ἄσμενος, ἥκων ἐξ ἀγροῦ. ἐπειδὴ δὲ ἦν
πρὸς ἡμέραν, ἧκεν ἐκείνη καὶ τὴν θύραν ἀνέῳξεν. ἐρομένου   40
δέ μου τί αἱ θύραι νύκτωρ ψοφοῖεν, ἔφασκε τὸν λύχνον
ἀποσβεσθῆναι τὸν παρὰ τῷ παιδίῳ, εἶτα ἐκ τῶν γειτόνων
ἐνάψασθαι. ἐσιώπων ἐγὼ καὶ ταῦτα οὕτως ἔχειν ἡγούμην.
ἔδοξε δέ μοι, ὦ ἄνδρες, τὸ πρόσωπον ἐψιμυθιῶσθαι, τοῦ
ἀδελφοῦ τεθνεῶτος οὔπω τριάκονθ᾽ ἡμέρας· ὅμως δ᾽ οὐδ᾽   45
οὕτως οὐδὲν εἰπὼν περὶ τοῦ πράγματος ἐξελθὼν ᾠχόμην ἔξω
σιωπῇ.

The *narratio* or *diegesis*
The whole set text is drawn from this part of the speech, the part in which the speaker sets out his version of the events involved in the case. Lysias was especially famed for the way in which he crafted this section of a speech: the plausibility of the account makes an important contribution to the overall persuasiveness of the speech. Lysias was particularly adept at introducing key details into the narrative – on which he would later build his argumentation – without giving them undue prominence. He was also able to convey the character of the individuals (*ethos*) effectively through his narrative which, as we have seen, was a key aspect of the persuasiveness of his speeches.

> Q. What impression do we get of Euphiletos' wife in this passage?
>
> Q. What is the effect of the use of direct speech in this section of the *narratio*?
>
> Q. Why do you think that Lysias is happy to leave the jury with the impression that Euphiletos had previously assaulted his slave-girl?
>
> Q. At the end of this section, how do you think that Lysias is trying to present the character of Euphiletos?

GCSE vocabulary: ἀγρός, ἀνήρ, ἀποθνήσκω, αὐτός, γε, γελάω, γυνή, διά (+ gen.), δοκεῖ, ἐγώ, ἐδώκα (δοῦναι), ἐθέλω, εἰμί, εἶμι (ἄπειμι), ἐκ/ἐξ, ἐκεῖνος, ἔρχομαι (ἐξῆλθον), ἐρωτάω (ἠρόμην), ἔχω, ἡμέρα, θύρα, ἵνα, καθεύδω, καί, κελεύω, λέγω (εἶπον), ὁράω, ὀργίζομαι, οὐ, οὐδείς, οὗτος, οὕτως, παύω, περί (+ gen.), πρός (+ acc.), πρότερον, πρῶτον, σύ, τίς, φημί (ἔφη), χρόνος, ὡς.

31 παιδίον – baby (see l.5).
32 τιτθός – breast; κλάω – cry.
33 ὡς ἂν – (supply οὐκ ἤθελε) 'as she would have been (unwilling)'; ἄσμενος -η -ον – glad (here translate adverbially with ἑωρακυῖα); ἑωρακυῖα (perfect participle active of ὁράω) – having seen: translate as conditional with ἀσμένη 'if she had been glad to see'; ἥκω – see l.27 (the participle with με forms an indirect statement); διὰ χρόνου – 'after some time'; ἐπειδή – when, since.
35 πειράω (> πειράομαι) (πειρᾷς is 2nd sing. present subjunctive) – have a go at, make a sexual advance towards; ἐνταῦθα – here; παιδίσκη ἡ (diminutive > παῖς) – slave-girl; μεθύω – be drunk.
36 ἕλκω (imperfect εἷλκον) – sexually assault, grope; κἀγώ = καὶ ἐγώ (crasis, see p.81); ἀναστᾶσα (fem. aorist participle of ἀνίσταμαι) – having stood up.
37 προστίθημι (3rd sing. προστίθησι, historic pres.) – close; προσποιέομαι (> ποιέω) – pretend; παίζω (> παῖς) – play.
38 κλείς -ιδός ἡ (acc. κλεῖν) – bolt; ἐφέλκομαι – fasten; ἐνθυμέομαι – take to heart, think much of, ponder; οὐδ' = οὐδέ (elision) – and . . . not.
39 ὑπονοέω – suspect; ἄσμενος – see l.33; ἥκω – see l.27; ἀγρός – country, countryside (see l.28); ἐπειδή – see l.33.
40 ἧκεν (imperfect of ἥκω) – see l.27; ἀνοίγνυμι (aorist ἀνέῳξα) – open.
41 τί – why (here); νύκτωρ (> νύξ) – during the night; ψοφέω – make a noise; φάσκω – say; λύχνος ὁ - lamp.
42 ἀποσβέννυμι (aor. passive ἀπεσβέσθην) – extinguish; παρά + dat. – beside; εἶτα = ἔπειτα; γείτων -ονος ὁ/ἡ – neighbour.
43 ἐνάπτομαι (aor. ἐνηψάμην) – get a light; σιωπάω – keep quiet; οὕτως ἔχειν – to be the case; ἡγέομαι – think, consider.
44 ἔδοξε – she seemed (here); πρόσωπον τό (< prosopopoeia) – face; ἐψιμυθιῶσθαι (perfect infinitive middle of ψιμυθιόομαι) – to have put white make-up on, to have whitened (with white lead).
46 ἀδελφός ὁ (< Philadelphia) – brother; τεθνεώς -ῶτος (masc. perfect participle of ἀποθνήσκω) – having died, having been dead; οὔπω (> οὐ) – not yet; τριάκονθ' = τριάκοντα (see l.15) – thirty (thirty days was the official period of mourning in Athens, during which female relatives of the dead would be expected to avoid wearing make-up); ὅμως – nevertheless; οὐδέ – not even: here it reinforces the following οὐδέν, translate as 'even'.
46 πρᾶγμα -ατος τό (> πράττω) – matter; οἴχομαι – go, be gone; ἔξω (> ἐξ) – outside, out.
47 σιωπή ἡ – silence.

After the previous passage, there is a very small gap in the set text, in which Euphiletos explains that he was subsequently waylaid outside his house by an old female slave of another woman whom Eratosthenes had seduced. The meeting leads Euphiletos to reappraise his wife's behaviour (Lysias 1. 16–18).

"Εὐφίλητε," ἔφη, "μηδεμιᾷ πολυπραγμοσύνῃ προσεληλυθέναι
με νόμιζε πρὸς σέ· ὁ γὰρ ἀνὴρ ὁ ὑβρίζων εἰς σὲ καὶ τὴν σὴν
γυναῖκα ἐχθρὸς ὢν ἡμῖν τυγχάνει. ἐὰν οὖν λάβῃς τὴν   50
θεράπαιναν τὴν εἰς ἀγορὰν βαδίζουσαν καὶ διακονοῦσαν ὑμῖν
καὶ βασανίσῃς, ἅπαντα πεύσει. ἔστι δ'," ἔφη, "Ἐρατοσθένης
Ὀῆθεν ὁ ταῦτα πράττων, ὃς οὐ μόνον τὴν σὴν γυναῖκα
διέφθαρκεν ἀλλὰ καὶ ἄλλας πολλάς· ταύτην γὰρ τὴν τέχνην
ἔχει." ταῦτα εἰποῦσα, ὦ ἄνδρες, ἐκείνη μὲν ἀπηλλάγη, ἐγὼ δ'   55
εὐθέως ἐταραττόμην, καὶ πάντα μου εἰς τὴν γνώμην εἰσῄει,
καὶ μεστὸς ἦν ὑποψίας, ἐνθυμούμενος μὲν ὡς ἀπεκλῄσθην ἐν
τῷ δωματίῳ, ἀναμιμνῃσκόμενος δὲ ὅτι ἐν ἐκείνῃ τῇ νυκτὶ
ἐψόφει ἡ μέταυλος θύρα καὶ ἡ αὔλειος, ὃ οὐδέποτε ἐγένετο,
ἔδοξέ τέ μοι ἡ γυνὴ ἐψιμυθιῶσθαι. ταῦτά μου πάντα εἰς τὴν   60
γνώμην εἰσῄει, καὶ μεστὸς ἦ ὑποψίας.

ἐλθὼν δὲ οἴκαδε ἐκέλευον ἀκολουθεῖν μοι τὴν θεράπαιναν εἰς
τὴν ἀγοράν, ἀγαγὼν δ' αὐτὴν ὡς τῶν ἐπιτηδείων τινὰ ἔλεγον
ὅτι ἐγὼ πάντα εἴην πεπυσμένος τὰ γιγνόμενα ἐν τῇ οἰκίᾳ·

Names and places

Εὐφίλητος ὁ: Euphiletos, *the defendant (this is the only place where we are told his name)*.

Ἐρατοσθένης -ους ὁ: Eratosthenes, *the man Euphiletos is on trial for killing.*

Ὀῆθεν: from Oe, *a deme, or district, of Attica; its exact location is uncertain. Giving a man's deme with his name was the normal way of identifying a citizen.*

Slaves

Several slaves feature in this speech, and some seem to be very close to their masters and mistresses. We have seen that the 'market' slave-woman was trusted to act as an intermediary between Euphiletos' wife and her lover, and here another slave-woman is given a very sensitive message to take to Euphiletos. Moreover, according to the speech, she has no hesitation in advising Euphiletos to use torture on his slave-woman to extract the truth. Indeed, torture was the usual method for extracting evidence from slaves in legal trials in Athens. Slavery was an institution which normalised the brutal treatment of other humans, but that did not, in other contexts, preclude very close relationships between slaves and their masters.

GCSE vocabulary: ἀγορά, ἄγω, ἀλλά, ἄλλος, ἀνήρ, αὐτόν, γάρ, γίγνομαι, γυνή, διαφθείρω, δοκεῖ, ἐάν, ἐγώ, εἰμί, εἶμι (εἴσειμι), εἰς, ἐκεῖνος, ἐν, ἔρχομαι (ἦλθον), ἐχθρός, ἔχω, θύρα, ἡμεῖς, καί, κελεύω, λαμβάνω, λέγω (εἶπον), μέν... δέ..., μηδείς, μόνον, νομίζω, νύξ, οἰκία, ὅς, ὅτι, οὐ, οὐδέποτε, οὖν, οὗτος, πᾶς, πολύς, πράττω, πρός (+ acc.), πυνθάνομαι, σός, σύ, τις, ὑμεῖς, φημί.

48 ἔφη – *the old slave-woman who has accosted Euphiletos in the street is speaking here*; **μηδεμιᾶ** – *this form of the negative is used because of the following imperative* νόμιζε: *translate as* 'do not think that ... from any ...'; πολυπραγμοσύνη (> πολύς & πράττω) – meddlesomeness; προσεληλυθέναι (*perfect infinitive of* προσέρχομαι) – to have approached.
49 ὑβρίζω εἰς + *acc.* (< hubristic) – commit an outrage against.
50 τυγχάνω (> τύχη) + *participle* (ὤν *here*) – happen to (be).
51 θεράπαινα – slave-woman; βαδίζω – walk, go; διακονέω + *dat.* – serve.
52 βασανίζω (*aor.* ἐβασάνισα) – torture; ἅπαντα – *see l.30.*
54 διέφθαρκεν (*3rd sing. perfect active of* διαφθείρω) – has corrupted; τέχνη ἡ (< technical) – skill.
55 ἀπηλλάγη (*3rd sing. aorist of* ἀπαλλάσσομαι) – departed.
56 εὐθέως = εὐθύς; ταράττω – throw into confusion; γνώμη ἡ – mind; εἰσῄει – *3rd sing. imperfect of* εἴσειμι.
57 μεστός -ή -όν + *gen.* – full; ἦν – *1st sing. imperfect of* εἰμί; ὑποψία ἡ – suspicion; ἐνθυμέομαι – take to heart, think much of, ponder; ὡς = ὅτι; ἀποκλῄω (*aorist passive* ἀπεκλῄσθην) – lock away.
58 δωμάτιον τό – room; ἀναμιμνῄσκομαι – remember.
59 ψοφέω – make a noise; μέταυλος -ον – inner (*between house and courtyard*): *note that this and the next adjective are two-termination, with no separate feminine form*; αὔλειος -ον – outer (*between yard and street*); ὅ – *neuter of* ὅς, *referring to the whole previous clause: translate as* 'a thing which'.
60 ἔδοξέ... ἐψιμυθιῶσθαι – *see l.44*; τε – *see l.4*; ταῦτά μου... ὑποψίας – *see lines 56–7.*
62 οἴκαδε (> οἰκία) – (to) home; ἀκολουθέω + *dat.* (< anacolouthon) – follow.
63 ὡς + *acc.* – to (*see l.22*); ἐπιτήδειος ὁ - close friend.
64 εἴην πεπυσμένος (*1st sing. perfect optative of* πυνθάνομαι) – *translate as* 'I had found out'.

Q. What reasons do you think Lysias has for giving the words of the slave-woman here as direct speech?
Q. Why does Lysias make Euphiletos repeat two clauses in lines 56–7 and 60–1?
Q. Why does Euphiletos take the slave-woman to a friend's house for questioning?

Euphiletos threatens the slave-woman who eventually reveals everything that has happened (Lysias 1. 18–20).

"σοὶ οὖν," ἔφην, "ἔξεστι δυοῖν ὁπότερον βούλει ἑλέσθαι, ἢ 65
μαστιγωθεῖσαν εἰς μύλωνα ἐμπεσεῖν καὶ μηδέποτε παύσασθαι
κακοῖς τοιούτοις συνεχομένην, ἢ κατειποῦσαν ἅπαντα τἀληθῆ
μηδὲν παθεῖν κακόν, ἀλλὰ συγγνώμης παρ' ἐμοῦ τυχεῖν
τῶν ἡμαρτημένων. ψεύσῃ δὲ μηδέν, ἀλλὰ πάντα τἀληθῆ λέγε."
κἀκείνη τὸ μὲν πρῶτον ἔξαρνος ἦν, καὶ ποιεῖν ἐκέλευεν ὅ τι 70
βούλομαι· οὐδὲν γὰρ εἰδέναι· ἐπειδὴ δὲ ἐγὼ ἐμνήσθην
Ἐρατοσθένους πρὸς αὐτήν, καὶ εἶπον ὅτι οὗτος ὁ φοιτῶν εἴη
πρὸς τὴν γυναῖκα, ἐξεπλάγη ἡγησαμένη με πάντα ἀκριβῶς
ἐγνωκέναι. καὶ τότε ἤδη πρὸς τὰ γόνατά μου πεσοῦσα, καὶ
πίστιν παρ' ἐμοῦ λαβοῦσα μηδὲν πείσεσθαι κακόν, κατηγόρει 75
πρῶτον μὲν ὡς μετὰ τὴν ἐκφορὰν αὐτῇ προσίοι, ἔπειτα ὡς
αὐτὴ τελευτῶσα εἰσαγγείλειε καὶ ὡς ἐκείνη τῷ χρόνῳ πεισθείη,
καὶ τὰς εἰσόδους οἷς τρόποις προσίοιτο, καὶ ὡς Θεσμοφορίοις
ἐμοῦ ἐν ἀγρῷ ὄντος ᾤχετο εἰς τὸ ἱερὸν μετὰ τῆς μητρὸς τῆς
ἐκείνου· καὶ τἆλλα τὰ γενόμενα πάντα ἀκριβῶς διηγήσατο. 80

Name
Θεσμοφόρια τά: the Thesmophoria, *a religious festival in honour of Demeter celebrated by Athenian women in October each year.*

The Thesmophoria
This was a women-only religious festival celebrated across Greece in autumn before the time of sowing. In honour of Demeter and her daughter Kore, it was one of several festivals concerned with fertility, and was linked to the time of sowing (just as there were others concerned with ploughing and the harvest). Apart from the fact that it lasted for three days, and involved throwing pigs into pits to let them rot, little is known about the festival. However, because it was for women only, it clearly played to the fears and insecurities of Athenian males as to what their women got up to when they were not around to control them. Aristophanes sets his play *Thesmophoriazusae* at the festival, and imagines the women there taking the opportunity to plot revenge against Euripides for all his allegedly misogynistic plays. In our speech it supposedly offered the chance for Euphiletos' wife to meet up with her lover's mother.

Q. How do you think the Athenian jury would have reacted to Euphiletos' threat to send the slave-woman to work in a mill?

Q. What finally convinces the slave-woman to talk?

Q. What does it suggest about the affair if Euphiletos' wife really was meeting up with her lover's mother at a religious festival? Why do you think this detail is included by Lysias?

GCSE vocabulary: ἀγρός, αἱρέω, ἀληθής, ἀλλά, ἄλλος, αὐτός, βούλομαι, γάρ, γίγνομαι, γιγνώσκω, γυνή, δύο, ἐγώ, εἰμί, εἶμι (πρόσειμι), εἰς, ἐκεῖνος, ἔξεστι, ἔπειτα, ἤ... ἤ..., ἤδη, ἱερόν, καί, κακός, κελεύω, λαμβάνω, λέγω (εἶπον), μέν... δέ..., μετά (+ acc.), μετά (+ gen.), μηδείς, μηδέποτε, μήτηρ, οἶδα (εἰδέναι), ὅς, ὅτι, οὐδείς, οὖν, οὗτος, παρά (+ gen.), πᾶς, πάσχω, παύω, πείθω, πίπτω (ἐμπίπτω), ποιέω, πρός (+ acc.), πρῶτον, σύ, τοιοῦτος, τότε, φημί, χρόνος, ὡς.

65 ὁπότερος -α -ον – which (of two); βούλει (= βούλῃ) – you wish; ἑλέσθαι (*aorist infinitive middle of* αἱρέω) – to choose.

66 μαστιγωθεῖσαν (*aorist participle passive of* μαστιγόω) – having been whipped (*fem. accusative singular, as if* σέ *rather than* σοί *had preceded in l.65*); μυλών -ῶνος ὁ – mill; ἐμπεσεῖν (*aor. inf. of* ἐμπίπτω) – to be thrown into.

67 συνέχομαι (> ἔχω) – be afflicted; καταλέγω (*aorist* κατεῖπον) – relate; ἅπαντα – see l.30; τἀληθῆ = τὰ ἀληθῆ (crasis, see p.81) – the truth.

68 συγγνώμη ἡ (> γιγνώσκω) – forgiveness; τυγχάνω (*aorist* ἔτυχον) + gen. (> τύχη) – meet with.

69 τῶν ἡμαρτημένων (*perfect passive participle of* ἁμαρτάνω) – translate as 'for your mistakes' (*genitive dependent on* συγγνώμης); ψεύδομαι (*aorist* ἐψευσάμην) (< pseudonym) – tell a lie (*the 2nd sing. subjunctive is expressing a negative command with* μηδέν); τἀληθῆ – see l.67.

70 κἀκείνη = καὶ ἐκείνη (crasis, see p.81); τὸ πρῶτον = πρῶτον; ἔξαρνος -ον – denying, in denial; ὅ τι – what (see l.3).

71 εἰδέναι – *infinitive of* οἶδα: *this is an indirect statement, following the indirect command in the previous line, with the verb of 'saying' understood: add* 'she said that she ...'; ἐπειδή – when, since; μιμνῄσκομαι (*aorist* ἐμνήσθην) + gen. – mention.

72 φοιτάω – visit frequently.

73 ἐκπλήσσω (*aorist passive* ἐξεπλάγην) – shock, astound; ἡγέομαι – think, consider; ἀκριβῶς – exactly, precisely.

74 ἐγνωκέναι (*perfect infinitive of* γιγνώσκω) – translate as 'had found out'; πρός + acc. – at (here); γόνυ -ατος τό – knee.

75 πίστις -εως ἡ (> πιστεύω) – pledge; πείσεσθαι – *fut. inf. of* πάσχω *in indirect statement after* πίστιν; κατηγορέω (< category) – accuse, denounce.

76 ὡς = ὅτι (*as repeatedly in lines 76–8*); ἐκφορά – funeral (see l.11); αὐτή – *refers to the slave-woman*.

77 τελευτῶσα (*participle from* τελευτάω – end, finish) – translate as 'finally'; εἰσαγγέλλω (> ἀγγέλλω) – act as go-between; ἐκείνη – *refers to his wife*.

78 εἴσοδος ἡ (> ὁδός) – entrance (*note the variation in construction:* τὰς εἰσόδους *follows* κατηγόρει *as a direct object, parallel to the* ὡς *clauses*); τρόπος ὁ – way, means; προσίοιτο (*3rd sing. pres. opt. pass. of* προσίημι) – translate as 'he was admitted'.

79 ἀγρός – see l.28; οἴχομαι – go, be gone.

80 τἆλλα = τὰ ἄλλα (crasis, see p.81); ἀκριβῶς – see l.73; διηγέομαι – explain, give an account of (see l.16).

Euphiletos is keen to catch the adulterer red-handed (Lysias 1. 21–3).

ἐπειδὴ δὲ πάντα εἴρητο αὐτῇ, εἶπον ἐγώ, "ὅπως τοίνυν ταῦτα μηδεὶς ἀνθρώπων πεύσεται· εἰ δὲ μή, οὐδέν σοι κύριον ἔσται τῶν πρὸς ἔμ' ὡμολογημένων. ἀξιῶ δέ σε ἐπ' αὐτοφώρῳ ταῦτά μοι ἐπιδεῖξαι· ἐγὼ γὰρ οὐδὲν δέομαι λόγων, ἀλλὰ τὸ ἔργον φανερὸν γενέσθαι, εἴπερ οὕτως ἔχει." ὡμολόγει ταῦτα   85
ποιήσειν. καὶ μετὰ ταῦτα διεγένοντο ἡμέραι τέτταρες ἢ πέντε καὶ ἐπ' αὐτοφώρῳ τὸν μοιχὸν ἔνδον ἔλαβον, ὡς ἐγὼ μεγάλοις ὑμῖν τεκμηρίοις ἐπιδείξω. πρῶτον δὲ διηγήσασθαι βούλομαι τὰ πραχθέντα τῇ τελευταίᾳ ἡμέρᾳ. Σώστρατος ἦν μοι ἐπιτήδειος καὶ φίλος. τούτῳ ἡλίου δεδυκότος ἰόντι ἐξ ἀγροῦ ἀπήντησα.   90
εἰδὼς δ' ἐγὼ ὅτι τηνικαῦτα ἀφιγμένος οὐδένα καταλήψοιτο οἴκοι τῶν ἐπιτηδείων, ἐκέλευον συνδειπνεῖν· καὶ ἐλθόντες οἴκαδε ὡς ἐμέ, ἀναβάντες εἰς τὸ ὑπερῷον ἐδειπνοῦμεν. ἐπειδὴ δὲ καλῶς αὐτῷ εἶχεν, ἐκεῖνος μὲν ἀπιὼν ᾤχετο, ἐγὼ δ' ἐκάθευδον.

Name
Σώστρατος ὁ: Sostratos, *a friend of Euphiletos.*

Catching an adulterer
It seems strange that Euphiletos should want to catch Eratosthenes in flagrante with his wife, rather than just put an end to the affair at the earliest possible opportunity. However, this is almost certainly connected with the terms of the law about adultery. For while it allowed the aggrieved party to seek other forms of redress from the adulterer, it also permitted the cuckolded husband to kill the adulterer if he caught him in the act of adultery with his wife: it is clear that Euphiletos wanted to extract the most extreme form of vengeance possible.

Sostratos
The Sostratos episode is the clearest example of one that at first sight appears to bear no relevance to the key points at issue in the *narratio*. However, its significance will become clear when Lysias sets out his arguments in the second half of the speech: there he will claim that it is extremely unlikely that, had he been planning to murder Eratosthenes unprovoked that evening, he would have invited a friend round for dinner beforehand; and that if he had, he would then not have sent him away, but rather have kept him there to serve as a witness to the fact that the homicide was justifiable. Do you find this a convincing argument?

> Q. Why does the slave-woman have to promise to tell nobody of her agreement with Euphiletos?
>
> Q. Why do you think Lysias expresses the delay of some days in the way in which he does?
>
> Q. What impression of Euphiletos do we get from his behaviour towards his friend Sostratos?

> **GCSE vocabulary:** ἀγρός, ἀλλά, ἄνθρωπος, αὐτόν, ἀφικνέομαι, βαίνω (ἀναβαίνω), βούλομαι, γάρ, γίγνομαι, ἐγώ, εἰ, εἰμί, εἶμι (ἄπειμι), εἰς, ἐκεῖνος, ἐξ, ἔργον, ἔρχομαι (ἦλθον), ἔχω, ἡ, ἡμέρα, καθεύδω, καί, καλός, κελεύω, λαμβάνω, λέγω (εἶπον), λόγος, μέγας, μέν... δέ..., μετά (+ acc.), μή, μηδείς, οἶδα (εἰδώς), ὅτι, οὐδείς, οὗτος, οὕτως, πᾶς, πέντε, ποιέω, πράττω, πρός (+ acc.), πρῶτον, πυνθάνομαι, σύ, τέτταρες, ὑμεῖς, φίλος, ὡς.

81 ἐπειδή – when, since; εἴρητο (*3rd sing. pluperfect passive of* λέγω) – had been said; αὐτῇ – by her (*dative of agent*); ὅπως (*used with future to express a strong exhortation or prohibition*) – see to it that; τοίνυν – well then.

82 πεύσεται – *3rd sing. future of* πυνθάνομαι; εἰ δὲ μή – otherwise; κύριος -α -ον – valid.

83 ὡμολογημένος -η -ον (*perfect passive participle of* ὁμολογέω) – having been agreed; ἀξιῶ (> ἄξιος) – demand, require; ἐπ' αὐτοφώρῳ (> αὐτός) – in the very act.

84 ἐπιδείκνυμι (*aorist* ἐπέδειξα) (< epideictic) – show; οὐδέν – not at all (*adverbial*); δέομαι + *genitive or* + *infinitive* – need, want.

85 φανερός -ά -όν (> φαίνομαι) – clear, manifest; εἴπερ – if indeed, if really; οὕτως ἔχειν – *see l.43*; ὁμολογέω – *see l.83*.

86 διαγίγνομαι (> γίγνομαι) – pass, elapse.

87 ἐπ' αὐτοφώρῳ – *see l.83*; μοιχός ὁ – adulterer; ἔνδον – inside, in the house.

88 τεκμήριον τό – proof; ἐπιδείξω (*future of* ἐπιδείκνυμι) – *see l.84*; διηγέομαι – explain, give an account of (*see l.16*).

89 τελευταῖος -α -ον (> τέλος) – last, final; ἐπιτήδειος – close friend.

90 ἥλιος ὁ – sun; δεδυκότος (*masc. gen. sing. of the perfect participle of* δύω) – having set; ἀγρός – *see l.28*; ἀπαντάω + *dat.* – meet.

91 ὅτι – *introduces indirect statement after* εἰδώς; τηνικαῦτα – at that hour; ἀφιγμένος (*perfect participle of* ἀφικνέομαι) – having arrived; καταλαμβάνω (*future* καταλήψομαι) (> λαμβάνω) – find.

92 οἴκοι (> οἰκία) – at home; ἐπιτήδειος – *see l.89*; συνδειπνέω (> δεῖπνον) – dine with.

93 οἴκαδε – (to) home (*see l.62*); ὡς + *acc.* – to (*see l.22*): translate ὡς ἐμέ as 'to my house'; ἀναβάντες – the men's room (andron) is now upstairs (*see l.20*); ὑπερῷον τό – upper floor; δειπνέω – dine; ἐπειδή - *see l.81*.

94 καλῶς ἔχειν – to be good (*compare l.43*): translate καλῶς αὐτῷ εἶχεν as 'all was well with him'; οἴχομαι – go, be gone.

Eratosthenes is caught and matters reach a dramatic conclusion (Lysias 1. 23–5).

ὁ δ' Ἐρατοσθένης, ὦ ἄνδρες, εἰσέρχεται, καὶ ἡ θεράπαινα   95
ἐπεγείρασά με εὐθὺς φράζει ὅτι ἔνδον ἐστί. κἀγὼ εἰπὼν
ἐκείνῃ ἐπιμελεῖσθαι τῆς θύρας, καταβὰς σιωπῇ ἐξέρχομαι,
καὶ ἀφικνοῦμαι ὡς τὸν καὶ τόν, καὶ τοὺς μὲν οὐκ ἔνδον
κατέλαβον, τοὺς δὲ οὐδ' ἐπιδημοῦντας ηὗρον. παραλαβὼν δ'
ὡς οἷον τ' ἦν πλείστους ἐκ τῶν παρόντων ἐβάδιζον. καὶ   100
δᾷδας λαβόντες ἐκ τοῦ ἐγγύτατα καπηλείου εἰσερχόμεθα,
ἀνεῳγμένης τῆς θύρας καὶ ὑπὸ τῆς ἀνθρώπου
παρεσκευασμένης. ὤσαντες δὲ τὴν θύραν τοῦ δωματίου οἱ
μὲν πρῶτοι εἰσιόντες ἔτι εἴδομεν αὐτὸν κατακείμενον παρὰ
τῇ γυναικί, οἱ δ' ὕστερον ἐν τῇ κλίνῃ γυμνὸν ἑστηκότα. ἐγὼ   105
δ', ὦ ἄνδρες, πατάξας καταβάλλω αὐτόν, καὶ τὼ χεῖρε
περιαγαγὼν εἰς τοὖπισθεν καὶ δήσας ἠρώτων διὰ τί ὑβρίζει
εἰς τὴν οἰκίαν τὴν ἐμὴν εἰσιών. κἀκεῖνος ἀδικεῖν μὲν
ὡμολόγει, ἠντεβόλει δὲ καὶ ἱκέτευε μὴ ἀποκτεῖναι ἀλλ'
ἀργύριον πράξασθαι.   110

Witnesses

Lysias is keen to emphasise the lengths to which Euphiletos went in order to ensure that he had witnesses to the adultery and revenge. Witnesses were never particularly trusted in Athenian legal cases, since there was an assumption that they might be friends of one of the litigants, or had been bribed. However, Euphiletos cannot just rely on his own word that he had caught Eratosthenes in flagrante with his wife, and was therefore justified in killing him.

The confession

Similarly, it was not apparently necessary for an adulterer to confess to his crime in order for his homicide to be justified, but it helps Euphiletos to counter the claim that no adultery had taken place and that Eratosthenes had been lured into the house so that he could be killed for some other, illegitimate, reason. Indeed, to judge from the section of argument that follows in the second half of this speech, this seems to have been the main strand of the prosecution case against Euphiletos (although, of course, the prosecution speech does not actually survive).

Q. Why do you think that Lysias makes Euphiletos go into so much detail about the difficulties he faced in procuring witnesses?

Q. How does Lysias seek to make this a dramatic narrative?

Q. How is the desperation of Eratosthenes conveyed as he begs for his life?

> **GCSE vocabulary:** ἄγω (περιάγω), ἀδικέω, ἀλλά, ἀνήρ, ἄνθρωπος, ἀποκτείνω, αὐτόν, ἀφικνέομαι, βαίνω (καταβαίνω), βάλλω (καταβάλλω), γυνή, διὰ τί, ἐγώ, εἰμί, εἶμι (εἴσειμι), εἰς, ἐκ, ἐκεῖνος, ἐμός, ἐν, ἔρχομαι, ἐρωτάω, ἔτι, εὐθύς, εὑρίσκω, θύρα, καί, λαμβάνω, λέγω (εἶπον), μέν... δέ..., μή, οἰκία, οἷος τ' εἰμί, ὁράω (εἶδον), ὅτι, οὐ, παρασκευάζω, πάρειμι, πολύς (πλεῖστος), πράττω, πρῶτος, ὑπό (+ gen.), ὕστερον, χείρ, ὡς.

95 εἰσέρχεται – *historic present, as are many main verbs here;* θεράπαινα – slave-woman.
96 ἐπεγείρω (*aorist* ἐπήγειρα) – wake up; φράζω – say; ἔνδον – inside, in the house; κἀγώ (= καὶ ἐγώ) – *see l.36.*
97 ἐπιμελέομαι + *gen.* – take care of; σιωπή – silence.
98 ὡς + *acc.* – to the house of (*see l.93*); τὸν καὶ τόν – this man and that; ἔνδον – *see l.96.*
99 καταλαμβάνω – find; οὐδ' = οὐδέ (*elision*) – not even; ἐπιδημέω (> δῆμος) – be in town; παραλαμβάνω (> λαμβάνω) – take with (me).
100 ὡς οἷον τ' ἦν πλείστους – 'as many as was possible'; βαδίζω – walk, go.
101 δᾷς δᾳδός ἡ – torch; ἐγγύτατα – nearest (*indeclinable*); καπηλεῖον τό – inn, tavern.
102 ἀνεῳγμένης (*fem. gen. sing. of perfect participle pass. of* ἀνοίγνυμι) – having been opened; ἄνθρωπος ἡ – woman (*referring to the slave-woman*).
103 παρεσκευασμένης (*fem. gen. sing. of perfect participle pass. of* παρασκευάζω) – having been got ready; ὠθέω (*aorist* ἔωσα) – push open, force; δωμάτιον – room.
104 κατάκειμαι (*participle* κατακείμενος) – lie; παρά + *dat.* – beside.
105 κλίνη ἡ (< recline) – bed; γυμνός -η -ον (< gymnasium) – naked; ἑστηκώς -ότος – standing.
106 πατάσσω (*aorist* ἐπάταξα) – strike, punch; καταβάλλω – knock down; τὼ χεῖρε (*dual accusative form of* ἡ χείρ, *see p.59*) – 'his (two) hands'.
107 εἰς τοὔπισθεν (= εἰς τὸ ὄπισθεν, crasis, *see p.81*) – 'behind his back' (*literally* 'to the back'); δέω (< asyndeton) – bind, tie; ὑβρίζω – *see l.49.*
108 κἀκεῖνος = καὶ ἐκεῖνος (crasis).
109 ὁμολογέω – agree (*see l.83*); ἀντιβολέω – entreat (*note the unusual double augment in the imperfect* ἠντεβόλει); ἱκετεύω – beg.
110 ἀργύριον τό – money; πράττομαι – exact, demand (for oneself).

Euphiletos delivers a speech as he administers justice to Eratosthenes (Lysias 1. 26–7).

ἐγὼ δ' εἶπον ὅτι "οὐκ ἐγώ σε ἀποκτενῶ, ἀλλ' ὁ τῆς πόλεως
νόμος, ὃν σὺ παραβαίνων περὶ ἐλάττονος τῶν ἡδονῶν
ἐποιήσω, καὶ μᾶλλον εἵλου τοιοῦτον ἁμάρτημα
ἐξαμαρτάνειν εἰς τὴν γυναῖκα τὴν ἐμὴν καὶ εἰς τοὺς
παῖδας τοὺς ἐμοὺς ἢ τοῖς νόμοις πείθεσθαι καὶ   115
κόσμιος εἶναι." οὕτως, ὦ ἄνδρες, ἐκεῖνος τούτων ἔτυχεν
ὧνπερ οἱ νόμοι κελεύουσι τοὺς τὰ τοιαῦτα πράττοντας.

Euphiletos' child

It is notable that in this section Euphiletos observes that the crime has been committed also against his own child, although it is worth noting that he uses the plural 'children' to exaggerate the crime, and perhaps to generalise its impact. This is a point to which the speech returns at greater length in section 33 after the end of the prescribed text: there it is noted that adultery makes the parentage of any children from a marriage uncertain. Apart from the scandal involved, this uncertainty undermines the legitimacy of their claim to any subsequent inheritance: are they the genuine heirs of their father?

Figure 4 *The Athenian Agora, looking towards the Acropolis. Most trials in democratic Athens took place in and around the agora. This case, as one where the accused had claimed the defence of justifiable homicide, took place at the Delphinion near the Acropolis.*
Photo: Getty (Maximilian Müller).

> Q. Do you agree that Euphiletos was only following the law in killing Eratosthenes for his adultery?
> Q. Why do you think that Lysias repeats the word ἐμός in lines 114–15?
> Q. What does the last sentence really mean? Why do you think that Lysias avoids explicitly saying what Euphiletos did?

GCSE vocabulary: αἱρέω, ἀλλά, ἀνήρ, ἀποκτείνω, βαίνω, γυνή, ἐγώ, εἰμί, εἰς, ἐκεῖνος, ἐμός, ἡ, καί, κελεύω, λέγω (εἶπον), μᾶλλον, νόμος, ὀλίγος (ἐλάττων), ὅς, ὅτι, οὐ, οὗτος, παῖς, πείθομαι, περί (+ gen.), ποιέω, πόλις, πράττω, σύ, τοιοῦτος.

111 ὅτι – *this is redundant before direct speech, and best omitted in translation.*
112 παραβαίνω (> βαίνω) – transgress; περὶ ἐλάττονος ποιέομαι – regard as less important; ἡδονή ἡ (> ἡδύς) – pleasure (τῶν ἡδονῶν *is a genitive of comparison, after* ἐλάττονος).
113 ἐποιήσω – *2nd sing. aor. middle of* ποιέω (*see above*); εἵλου – *for the meaning of the middle of* αἱρέω, *see l.65*; ἁμάρτημα τό – offence, crime.
114 ἐξαμαρτάνω – commit (*note this verb is cognate with* ἁμάρτημα); εἰς + *acc.* – against (*here*).
115 ἤ – than (*this follows* μᾶλλον *in l.113*).
116 κόσμιος -α -ον (< cosmology) – well-behaved, honest; τυγχάνω – *see l.68.*
117 ὧνπερ – *from* ὅσπερ, *a strengthened form of* ὅς: *translate as* 'the very things which' (*the genitive is dependent on an infinitive* τυχεῖν, *which needs to be supplied after* κελεύουσι *from* ἔτυχεν *in the main clause*).

Figure 5 *Prothesis of body before an Athenian funeral. Black-figure terracotta funerary plaque, Greek, Attic, c. 520–510 BCE. Observe the participation of female figures here, just like the involvement of the wife of Euphiletos in his mother's funeral procession.*
Photo: Metropolitan Museum of Art, 54.11.5, Rogers Fund, 1954.

What happens next?

Euphiletos goes on to deny that Eratosthenes had been snatched off the street or had sought refuge at the hearth, as the prosecution had claimed. Then he turns to the adultery law in order to show that his vengeance was justified, before calling witnesses to support his account of Eratosthenes' death. He also notes – shockingly for modern readers – that the law concerned with adultery was more severe in its penalties than the one concerned with rape: the 'logic' was that adulterers corrupted the minds of the women, whereas rapists only used violence on the bodies of their female victims.

Euphiletos then proceeds to claim that the law did not just permit him to kill Eratosthenes, but ordered it, and that it is up to the jury to ensure by their verdict that the laws remain valid. He uses humour to note that if the jury finds him guilty, they will be inviting an open season for adulterers, even to the extent that burglars when caught in a house will claim that they are committing adultery in order to escape scot-free. He then rebuts in turn each of what he claims were the arguments of the prosecution, in particular relying on the Sostratos episode, and the difficulty he had in obtaining witnesses, to demonstrate that he had not plotted in advance to kill Eratosthenes that night. He restates that he had no other motive to kill the man; indeed, he claims never to have seen him before the night in question.

He concludes in a manner which follows the advice of ancient rhetorical manuals, namely by broadening the relevance of the case. He claims to have exacted vengeance not just for himself, but for the city as a whole, since his actions will have acted as a deterrent to other potential adulterers. If the jury finds him guilty it will overturn the existing system of justice, since he claims that, in future, citizens will be frightened to follow the laws, as trials will seem to offer more to fear for the law-abiding rather than for the criminals. He ends by restating how much is at stake for him.

We do not know the outcome of the trial, though it is normally assumed that it must have resulted in an acquittal since the speech took the prominent first position in the collection of Lysias' published speeches: why would a logographer advertise a failure? Even more difficult to ascertain is whether Eratosthenes was killed legally: if any entrapment had been involved in luring him into Euphiletos' house, then it was murder.

Final questions

- Which parts of the speech that you have read do you find most convincing, and which parts less so?
- What alternative narratives can you construct to undermine the account of events provided by Lysias' speech?
- How successfully do you think that Lysias creates an impression of Euphiletos which would have appealed to the Athenian jurors?
- Carey (a modern commentator on the speech) says of Eratosthenes that 'he does not emerge as a distinct personality'. Do you agree? If so, why do you think that may be the case?
- What overall picture of life for women in ancient Athens is revealed by the parts of the speech which you have read?
- Would you have acquitted or convicted Euphiletos?

Homer

The *Iliad* and *Odyssey* emerged in their current form probably towards the end of the eighth century. Whether there was a person called Homer and whether both works were by the same author or authors have been disputed for well over 2,000 years. In many ways, these questions do not matter. The poems have been read and appreciated over the centuries for their deep understanding of human nature both in what the characters say and in how they act.

We do know that the epics were produced at the end of a long oral tradition of bards who composed their verse songs of heroes, without the use of writing, in dactylic hexameters (the meter also of the *Iliad* and *Odyssey*, which has six stressed syllables in each line). These storytellers performed their compositions from memory or through improvisation before audiences and handed them down across the generations. It is this long tradition which helped to develop such an extensive system of epithets for the different heroes depending on which grammatical case they appeared in on each occasion, and how much of the line needed to be filled (on these epithets, see below p. 62). The poems themselves reflect the existence of such bards and particularly in the *Odyssey*, we see bards perform and extemporise tales of gods and heroes, accompanying themselves on the lyre. The context for such performances was usually a feast or celebration, just as happens when Odysseus is being entertained by the Phaeacians in book 8.

The two key differences between such performances and the two surviving epics are scale and complexity. While we know of other poems based on episodes from the Trojan War from the same period, none of them survived, none approached the length of the two surviving epics, nor did any of them show the same sophistication of overall structure or control of pace and shape. Although the *Iliad* is ostensibly about a short period during the final year of the Trojan War, and most of its action takes place over just three days, it encompasses a huge number of overarching themes of the war as a whole: heroism, friendship, enmity, death, the interactions of and differences between men and gods, the glory and suffering of war, and even the fate of the inhabitants of a captured city (Troy's capture is often foreshadowed, although it does not fall within the timescale of the epic).

The *Odyssey* is arguably even more complex in its structure and ambition, as, in addition to many of the themes which the *Iliad* explores, it can look back to the earlier epic and reflect on the 'celebrity status' that the heroes of that poem had won as the result of their glorious, and less glorious, deeds at Troy. Although it focuses on the extended journey home of one of those heroes, the returns of others, most notably Menelaus, Nestor and Agamemnon, also feature, and in combination these offer sustained reflection on the personal price, especially on the home front, that had to be paid by those who went off to fight. Moreover, Odysseus' journey through extraordinary lands, and his encounters with fantastical races, also offers the hero and the audience the opportunity to reflect on the nature of Greekness. For, although there was not yet a universal word for 'Greek' or 'Greece' at the time of its composition, the poem shows clear signs of thinking about what it was to be Greek, in terms of acceptable behaviour, especially in the realm of hospitality, shared cultural norms, and not least the collective mass of legends and stories, whose importance the *Odyssey* and *Iliad* themselves did so much to consolidate and establish.

Some features of Homeric Greek

The language of the Homeric poems differs from the Greek you have been studying for three reasons: it is verse, not prose; the language evolved over the centuries; and different regions had different dialects. 'Attic' Greek is the Greek spoken by the Athenians; the Homeric poems are largely in an Ionic dialect.

1. Elision

Where a word ends in a short vowel (mainly ε or α), it may drop this vowel in front of another word beginning with a vowel. This is marked with an apostrophe to show where the missing letter was, in the same way as in English: e.g. don't = do not. If the initial vowel of the second word is aspirated (has a rough breathing), the 'h' sound is repeated in the final consonants of the elided word (e.g. τ becomes θ', π becomes φ', κ becomes χ').

e.g.   μετ' = μετά (line 2)   δ' = δέ (3)   τίφθ' = τίπτε (97)

2. Uses of the article

In Homer the pronoun which became the definite article (ὁ ἡ τό) in Attic was used differently, either as a third person pronoun (an alternative to αὐτόν, such as τῷ in line 6), or as the relative pronoun (such as τούς in line 11), or as a demonstrative pronoun (such as τόν used for τοῦτον in line 88). The absence of the article in Homer means that it should be supplied when appropriate in translating (just as always in Latin).

3. Missing augments

In Attic Greek an augment shows an indicative verb is in a past tense. This was not yet a fixed convention when the Homeric poems were composed, although they are often used.

e.g.   ἄρχον = ἦρχον (3)   and   πάλλομεν = ἐπάλλομεν (4)

but compare ἠρίθμεον (2)

4. Uncontracted forms
Standard contractions are often left uncontracted.

 e.g. ἠρίθμεον = ἠρίθμουν (2) ἀδευκέα = ἀδευκῆ (43)

5. Tmesis (> τέμνω – *cut*)
In later Greek the preposition becomes attached as a prefix to the verb. This is often not the case in Homeric Greek, where you may find a prepositional prefix floating a word or two before the verb.

 e.g. ἐκ ... ἔθορε = ἐξέθορε (5) κατὰ ... λίπον = καταλίπον (7)

6. Alternative forms or words may exist side-by-side with more familiar ones

 e.g. ἠδέ = καί (10) ἔσκε = ἦν (46)

7. Homeric grammatical forms
Watch out especially for alternative infinitive forms, and for different genitive singular and dative plural endings.

Infinitives (ending -μεναι -or -εμεν)
  ἔδμεναι = ἔδειν (41)   φαγέμεν = φαγεῖν (105)

Genitive singular (2nd declension ending –οιο)
  Εὐρυλόχοιο = Εὐρυλόχου (5) μεγάροιο = μεγάρου (107)

Dative plurals: (ending –σι(ν))
  ἀμφοτέροισιν = ἀμφοτέροις (2) βήσσῃσι = βήσσαις (8)

In addition, in Ionic Greek, η is often found where we would expect α in Attic, such as in ἀγγελίην for ἀγγελίαν in line 43. In the vocabulary help the Ionic forms are given, rather than the equivalent Attic ones.

Homer also used dual forms more commonly than later Attic Greek. Duals were used instead of singular or plural forms when referring to precisely two things. At GCSE, the number δύο has dual forms, as by its very nature the number 'two' must always be dual. In this set text the dual form of 'we' is used by Circe of herself and Odysseus at line 75 (νῶϊ), where it is used with other duals, but also plural forms.

8. Diaeresis
Sometimes two vowels, normally sounded as one sound in a diphthong, were pronounced separately for the sake of the rhythm of the metrical scheme. This is indicated in the text by two dots over the second vowel.

 e.g. χαλκήρεϊ 4   ἀϊδρείῃσιν 29

2027–28 Prescription

This selection corresponds to Homer, *Odyssey* 10. 203–45; 302–47; 371–99.

The story so far

The word 'odyssey' has become a label for any long and eventful journey, metaphorical as well as actual, but the original *Odyssey* tells of the journey made by the famously cunning and enduring Odysseus back to his home in Ithaca, an island off the west coast of Greece, after the eventual Greek victory in the ten-year Trojan War.

The opening line of the epic begins with the poet appealing to the Muse to tell him of 'a man' (which is the very first word), and it is very much a poem about Odysseus. However, the remainder of the opening four books actually focus first on the gods, and then the deteriorating situation in Ithaca during Odysseus' long absence and his son Telemachus' attempt to find news of his father. The narrative begins in the tenth year of his return when he has been away from home for twenty years in total. At this point, the gods are divided, with Poseidon still desperately opposed to Odysseus' successful return, after the latter had blinded his son, the Cyclops Polyphemus, but the other gods, and especially Athene, feeling pity for him. Zeus sides with the majority and Athene makes plans to facilitate his return.

We finally encounter Odysseus in book 5, when he is crying on the shore of Calypso's remote and fantastical island of Ogygia, thinking about his home life in Ithaca and despairing of his return. Calypso is a minor goddess who had saved Odysseus when his ship had been wrecked in a storm and he had been carried to her island. She had looked after him, taken him as her lover, and kept him on the island for seven years. However, Hermes, sent by Zeus, forced her to assist Odysseus' escape and she helped him to build and stock a raft.

Poseidon, however, still furious, catches sight of Odysseus at sea again and sends a storm to wreck his raft, although he is unable to prevent his escape to the island of Scherie, where the Phaeacians live. Here he is guided to King Alcinous' palace by his daughter, where he is hospitably entertained and promised safe return to Ithaca, before the king finally asks him about his identity and how he came to Scherie in such a state.

Books 9–12 are therefore almost entirely told in Odysseus' own voice as he narrates in flashback his adventures as he set out with twelve ships from Troy and struggled to reach home. Initially the geography is real when he and his men land first in Thrace and sack the city of Ismarus, but then a huge storm arises and blows them into a fantastical version of the Mediterranean full of monsters and magic. These books include some of the most famous stories of the epic, encompassing his encounters with the Lotus-Eaters and two races of man-eating giants, the Cyclopes and the Laestrygonians, all of which he escapes thanks to his cunning, although the last of these destroy all eleven of his other ships and kill their crews.

Our story follows straight after this, on the island of Aeaea, home of Circe, an enchantress and daughter of Helios (the Sun God). Landing with his one surviving ship and seeing smoke rising inland, Odysseus decides that they must investigate, despite his men's great reluctance following the traumas which they have recently suffered. As a precaution, Odysseus divides his remaining ship's crew into two parties.

Figure 6 *Drinking cup (black-figure kylix) depicting Circe transforming Odysseus' men, Greek, Attic, 550–525 BCE. Observe Odysseus rushing in from the left with his sword. How does this depiction of Circe and the transformation of the men differ from Homer's account?*
Photo: MFA Boston.

Figure 7 *Circe by Wright Barker (1889). Observe the lyre which Circe is shown holding. What are the key aspects of this depiction of Circe, and how faithful are they to the Homeric version?*
Photo: Art UK (Bradford Museums and Galleries).

After the drawing of lots, Eurylochus leads half of Odysseus' men to investigate Circe's house, where they encounter animals behaving strangely (Odyssey 10. 203–15)

αὐτὰρ ἐγὼ δίχα πάντας ἐϋκνήμιδας ἑταίρους
ἠρίθμεον, ἀρχὸν δὲ μετ' ἀμφοτέροισιν ὄπασσα·
τῶν μὲν ἐγὼν ἄρχον, τῶν δ' Εὐρύλοχος θεοειδής.
κλήρους δ' ἐν κυνέῃ χαλκήρεϊ πάλλομεν ὦκα·
ἐκ δ' ἔθορε κλῆρος μεγαλήτορος Εὐρυλόχοιο.   5
βῆ δ' ἰέναι, ἅμα τῷ γε δύω καὶ εἴκοσ' ἑταῖροι
κλαίοντες· κατὰ δ' ἄμμε λίπον γοόωντας ὄπισθεν.
εὗρον δ' ἐν βήσσῃσι τετυγμένα δώματα Κίρκης
ξεστοῖσιν λάεσσι, περισκέπτῳ ἐνὶ χώρῳ.
ἀμφὶ δέ μιν λύκοι ἦσαν ὀρέστεροι ἠδὲ λέοντες,   10
τοὺς αὐτὴ κατέθελξεν, ἐπεὶ κακὰ φάρμακ' ἔδωκεν.
οὐδ' οἵ γ' ὁρμήθησαν ἐπ' ἀνδράσιν, ἀλλ' ἄρα τοί γε
οὐρῇσιν μακρῇσι περισσαίνοντες ἀνέσταν.

Names
Εὐρύλοχος -ου ὁ: Eurylochus, *one of Odysseus' companions.*

Κίρκη -ης ἡ: Circe, *divine enchantress, living alone on the island of Aeaea.*

Homeric epithets

An important feature of the works of Homer is the use of stock epithets (adjectives), regularly applied to individuals, places or things. This usage arises from the oral origins of the epics: in order for the poet more easily to compose metrical lines as he was telling the story from memory, he used set formulae of noun-adjective pairs to fit the rhythm of the line, which were easy for the poet and audience to remember, for example, 'resourceful Odysseus'. The adjectives are often not particularly relevant to the context in which they are used. An example comes in the first line of this passage when Odysseus refers to his companions as 'well-greaved' (ἐϋκνήμιδας), at a moment when it is of no consequence for them to be wearing greaves at all. However, the repeated use of these epithets can add a grandeur and an epic colour to the narrative. Two different epithets are used of Eurylochus in this passage, 'god-like' (θεοειδής, line 3) and 'great-hearted' (μεγαλήτορος, line 5), as he appears in two different cases (nominative, then genitive) and the poet requires the noun-adjective pair to take up a different portion of the line in each case.

> Q. What is the effect of the two different epithets used of Eurylochus in this passage? Does our perception of either of them change when we have read the following narrative?
>
> Q. As Eurylochus leaves with his men, what does the weeping of both groups (line 7) suggest about Odysseus' companions at this point?
>
> Q. How does the behaviour of the animals in lines 10–13 create an air of mystery around Circe's house?

> **GCSE vocabulary:** ἀλλά, ἀνήρ, ἄρχω, αὐτός, γε, ἔβην (βαίνω), ἐγώ, ἔδωκα (δίδωμι), ἐν, ἐπεί, ἦν (εἰμί), ἦσαν (εἰμί), ηὗρον (εὑρίσκω), ἰέναι (ἔρχομαι), κακός, λείπω, μέν … δέ, πᾶς.

1 αὐτάρ – but, yet, now; δίχα (< dichotomy) – in two; ἐϋκνήμις -ιδος – well-greaved (*a greave is a piece of armour protecting the lower leg*); ἑταῖρος ὁ – companion.

2 ἀριθμέω (< arithmetic) – count, (with δίχα) divide (ἠρίθμεον, *see* Uncontracted forms, *p.59*); ἀρχός ὁ (> ἄρχω) – leader; μετ' (= μετά, *see* Elision, *p.58*) + dat. – among; ἀμφότερος -η -ον– both (ἀμφοτέροισιν = ἀμφοτέροις, see Homeric grammatical forms, *p.59*); ὀπάζω – give, assign (ὄπασσα – *aorist, see* Missing augments, *p.58, and compare* πάλλομεν *in line 4*).

3 τῶν μέν… τῶν δ' (οἱ μέν … οἱ δέ) – 'of one group … of the other'; ἐγών = ἐγώ; ἄρχον = ἦρχον (*imperfect of* ἄρχω: *note the difference of accent from the noun* ἀρχόν *in the previous line*); θεοειδής -ές (> θεός) – godlike, looking like a god; *supply* ἦρχε *as the verb with* Εὐρύλοχος *from* ἄρχον *in the first half of the line*.

4 κλῆρος ὁ – lot; κυνέη ἡ – helmet; χαλκήρης -ες – fitted with bronze; πάλλω – shake; ὦκα – quickly.

5 ἐκ … ἔθορε (*by* Tmesis, *p.59, from* ἐκθρώσκω, *aorist* ἐξέθορα) – leap out; μεγαλήτωρ -ορος – great-hearted; Εὐρυλόχοιο = Εὐρυλόχου (*see* Homeric grammatical forms, *p.59*).

6 βῆ = ἔβη: βῆ … ἰέναι – 'he made to go' (*literally* 'he went to go'); ἅμα + dat. – with, together with; τῷ = αὐτῷ (*see* Uses of the article, *p.58*) *emphasised by the following* γε; δύω = δύο; εἴκοσι – twenty; ἑταῖρος – see l.1.

7 κλαίω – cry, weep; κατά … λίπον, *by tmesis from* καταλείπω – leave behind; ἄμμε = ἡμᾶς; γοάω (*participle* γοῶν) – wail; ὄπισθεν – behind.

8 εὗρον = ηὗρον (*missing augment*); βῆσσα ἡ – glade, forest clearing (βήσσῃσι = βήσσαις, *poetic plural*); τετυγμένος -η -ον – built (*perfect participle passive of* τεύχω); δῶμα -ατος τό – house (*poetic plural*).

9 ξεστός -ή -όν – polished; λᾶας -ος ὁ – stone; περίσκεπτος -ον – far-seen, open to view; ἐνί = ἐν; χῶρος ὁ – place, spot.

10 ἀμφί + acc. – around; μιν = αὐτόν (*referring back to* χώρῳ); λύκος ὁ (< lycanthrope) – wolf; ὀρέστερος (> ὄρος) – mountain-dwelling; ἠδέ = καί; λέων -οντος ὁ – lion.

11 τούς (= οὕς, *see* Uses of the article, *p.58*) – which; καταθέλγω (*aorist* κατέθελξα) – enchant, bewitch; φάρμακον -ου τό (< pharmacy) – drug.

12 οὐδέ – and … not, but … not, nor; οἵ (*used for* οὗτοι) – they (*referring to the animals*); ὁρμάομαι (*unaugmented aor*. ὁρμήθην) – rush, charge; ἐπί + dat. (*compare* ἐπί + *acc*.) – at, against; ἄρα – indeed, actually: *in Homer* ἄρα *draws attention to a particular detail or event, but is often untranslatable*; τοι (= οἱ) – they; γε (*the second in the line*) – *this particle draws attention to the contrast with how the animals might be expected to behave* (*compare* οἵ γ' *in the first half of the line*), *but cannot easily be translated*.

13 οὐρή ἡ – tail; μακρός -ή -όν (< macron) – long; περισσαίνω – wag around, fawn upon; ἀνίσταμαι (*3rd plur. aorist*: ἀνέσταν) – rear up.

Afraid because of the strange animals, the men are reassured by the sound of Circe singing and Polites urges them to call out to her (Odyssey 10. 216–29).

ὡς δ' ὅτ' ἂν ἀμφὶ ἄνακτα κύνες δαίτηθεν ἰόντα
σαίνωσ'· αἰεὶ γάρ τε φέρει μειλίγματα θυμοῦ·   15
ὣς τοὺς ἀμφὶ λύκοι κρατερώνυχες ἠδὲ λέοντες
σαῖνον· τοὶ δ' ἔδεισαν, ἐπεὶ ἴδον αἰνὰ πέλωρα.
ἔσταν δ' ἐν προθύροισι θεᾶς καλλιπλοκάμοιο,
Κίρκης δ' ἔνδον ἄκουον ἀειδούσης ὀπὶ καλῇ,
ἱστὸν ἐποιχομένης μέγαν ἄμβροτον, οἷα θεάων   20
λεπτά τε καὶ χαρίεντα καὶ ἀγλαὰ ἔργα πέλονται.
τοῖσι δὲ μύθων ἄρχε Πολίτης, ὄρχαμος ἀνδρῶν,
ὅς μοι κήδιστος ἑτάρων ἦν κεδνότατός τε·
   'ὦ φίλοι, ἔνδον γάρ τις ἐποιχομένη μέγαν ἱστὸν
καλὸν ἀοιδιάει, δάπεδον δ' ἅπαν ἀμφιμέμυκεν,   25
ἢ θεὸς ἠὲ γυνή· ἀλλὰ φθεγγώμεθα θᾶσσον.'
   ὣς ἄρ' ἐφώνησεν, τοὶ δ' ἐφθέγγοντο καλεῦντες.

Name
Πολίτης ὁ: Polites, *one of Odysseus' companions*.

Homeric similes
The narrative of both Homeric epics is enlivened by the inclusion of similes, often of extended length, in which the image of the simile is often developed far beyond the initial point of comparison. The simile in lines 14–15 is relatively brief and clarifies the strangely fawning nature of the wild animals. However, even here it perhaps raises the question for the audience of whether there is an equivalent figure of 'the master' (ἄναξ) in the actual narrative.

The role of women
Women in Homer are strongly associated with the production and care of fabrics in the home: Penelope devises the ruse of weaving (and at night unpicking) a burial shroud for Laertes, in order to delay making a decision over which suitor to marry (*Od.* 2. 97–110), and Nausicaa, persuaded by Athene, goes to the seaside to wash her and her family's clothes in book 6. So here Circe is depicted as weaving, even though she is a goddess and living on her own.

Q.   In what sense are the animals 'monsters' (πέλωρα)?

Q.   What impression do we get of Circe from the way in which she is first introduced into the narrative?

Q.   What is the significance of the brief characterisation of Polites in lines 22–3, before he speaks?

> **GCSE vocabulary:** ἀεί, ἀκούω, ἀλλά, ἀνήρ, ἄρχω, γάρ, γυνή, ἐγώ, εἶδον (ὁράω), ἐν, ἐπεί, ἔργον, ἤ... ἤ, ἤν (εἰμί), θάσσων (ταχύς), θεά, ἰών (εἶμι), καλέω, καλός, μέγας, μοι (ἐγώ), μῦθος, ὅς, τε... καί, τις, φέρω, φίλος, ὦ, ὡς.

14 ὅτ' ἄν + *subjunctive* (σαίνωσι) – whenever, when (*the indefinite construction*): ὡς ὅτ' ἄν *often introduces a simile* ('just as when'); ἀμφί + *acc.* – around; ἄναξ -ακτος ὁ – lord, master; κύων -νός ὁ/ἡ – dog; δαίτηθεν – from a feast (> δαίς + -θεν, *a suffix meaning 'from'*).

15 σαίνω – wag (*compare* περισσαίνω *in l.13*); αἰεί = ἀεί; τε – *in Homer this particle is often, as here, used to mark a generalising statement: it cannot be translated*; φέρει – *the 'master' is now the subject*; μείλιγμα -ατος τό – that which soothes, appeasement; θυμός ὁ – heart, wrath, appetite.

16 ὥς – so, in this way (*often used to resume the narrative, after a simile*); τούς = αὐτούς (*referring to Eurylochus and his men, see* Uses of the article, *p.58*); ἀμφί – around (*here follows the accusative,* τούς, *to which it refers*); λύκος, ἠδέ *and* λέων – *see l.10*; κρατερῶνυξ -υχος – strong-clawed.

17 σαίνω – *see l.15: note omitted augment* (so also ἴδον = εἶδον); τοί = οἱ (*see l.12*), *referring to the men, and marking a change of subject*; δείδω (*aorist* ἔδεισα) – I fear; αἰνός -ή -όν – dreadful; πέλωρον τό – monster, beast.

18 ἔσταν (*3rd plur. aorist of* ἵσταμαι) – they stood; πρόθυρον τό (> πρό + θύρα) – porch, doorway (*poetic plural*); καλλιπλόκαμος -ον (> καλός) – of beautiful hair (*note that this adjective is two-termination and has no feminine form, like all compound adjectives: therefore, it agrees with* θεᾶς).

19 ἔνδον (< endogamy) – inside; ἀείδω – sing; ὄψ ὀπός ἡ – voice.

20 ἱστός ὁ – loom; ἐποίχομαι – go back and forth at, am busy at; ἀμβρυτος -ον – immortal, divine; οἷος -η -ον – such, of such a sort (*supply* 'weaving' *from* ἱστὸν ἐποιχομένης): *translate as* 'weaving such things as the ... works of goddesses usually are'; θεάων = θεῶν, *goes with* ἔργα.

21 λεπτός -ή -όν – delicate; χαρίεις -εσσα -εν – graceful; ἀγλαός -όν – shining, brilliant; πέλομαι – am, am usually.

22 τοῖσι = αὐτοῖς; μῦθος ὁ – speech (*poetic plural*); ἄρχω + *gen.* – begin (*here*); ὄρχαμος ὁ – leader.

23 κήδιστος -η -ον – dearest; ἔταρος (= ἑταῖρος) – companion (*see l.1*); κεδνός -ή -όν – cherished; τε – and (*placed, as always, after the word it is translated in front of*).

24 ἔνδον – *see l.19*; γάρ – *explains Polites' decision to address the men: translate as* 'certainly'; ἐποιχομένη μέγαν ἱστόν – *see l.20*.

25 καλόν – beautifully (*adverbial*); ἀοιδιάω = ἀείδω (*see l.19*); δάπεδον τό – ground; ἅπας -ασα -αν (> πᾶς) – all, whole; ἀμφιμέμυκεν – '(it) re-echoes' (*perfect with present meaning from* ἀμφιμυκάομαι).

26 ἤ... ἠέ = ἤ... ἤ; φθεγγώμεθα – 'let us speak up' (*jussive subjunctive of* φθέγγομαι); θᾶσσον – *translate the comparative as* 'rather quickly'.

27 ὥς – *see l.16*; ἄρ' = ἄρα (*by* Elision, *p.58*), *see l.12*; φωνέω (> φωνή) – speak; τοί = οἱ (*see l.12*); καλεῦντες = καλοῦντες.

Circe invites the men in and turns them into pigs while Eurylochus, who remained outside, reports what has happened to Odysseus (Odyssey 10. 230–45).

ἡ δ' αἶψ' ἐξελθοῦσα θύρας ὤϊξε φαεινὰς
καὶ κάλει· οἱ δ' ἅμα πάντες ἀϊδρείῃσιν ἕποντο·
Εὐρύλοχος δ' ὑπέμεινεν, ὀϊσάμενος δόλον εἶναι.   30
εἷσεν δ' εἰσαγαγοῦσα κατὰ κλισμούς τε θρόνους τε,
ἐν δέ σφιν τυρόν τε καὶ ἄλφιτα καὶ μέλι χλωρὸν
οἴνῳ Πραμνείῳ ἐκύκα· ἀνέμισγε δὲ σίτῳ
φάρμακα λύγρ', ἵνα πάγχυ λαθοίατο πατρίδος αἴης.
αὐτὰρ ἐπεὶ δῶκέν τε καὶ ἔκπιον, αὐτίκ' ἔπειτα   35
ῥάβδῳ πεπληγυῖα κατὰ συφεοῖσιν ἐέργνυ.
οἱ δὲ συῶν μὲν ἔχον κεφαλὰς φωνήν τε τρίχας τε
καὶ δέμας, αὐτὰρ νοῦς ἦν ἔμπεδος ὡς τὸ πάρος περ.
ὣς οἱ μὲν κλαίοντες ἐέρχατο· τοῖσι δὲ Κίρκη
πὰρ ῥ' ἄκυλον βάλανόν τ' ἔβαλεν καρπόν τε κρανείης   40
ἔδμεναι, οἷα σύες χαμαιευνάδες αἰὲν ἔδουσιν.
   Εὐρύλοχος δ' ἂψ ἦλθε θοὴν ἐπὶ νῆα μέλαιναν,
ἀγγελίην ἑτάρων ἐρέων καὶ ἀδευκέα πότμον.

Name
Πραμνείος -η -ον: Pramnian, *a variety of wine which was dark and strong.*

Magic in the *Odyssey*
Circe uses magic on Odysseus' men, giving them drugs to make them forget about their homes and turn them into pigs: although the men are described as still possessing their normal mental capacity, they have the form of pigs and are only able to grunt rather than speak. This is not the only time that drugs and magic are used in the epic: in book 9, those of Odysseus' men who eat the Lotus flowers lose all desire to head home, and in book 4, Helen (rather like Circe here) adds a drug to wine for Telemachus which provides forgetfulness of every kind of trouble. Athena in book 13 touches Odysseus with a stick to transform him into a beggar, a disguise to help him take vengeance on the suitors: this suggests that Circe's use of her stick (or wand) in this episode may also be part of her magic.

> Q. What is the significance of the many imperfects in this passage (in lines 29, 33 and 36–7)?
>
> Q. In what way does Circe's treatment of Odysseus' men follow the usual rules of hospitality and how does it transgress them?
>
> Q. Are Odysseus' men presented as naïve in this part of the story? Given that we have already met enchanted lions and wolves, is it significant that Odysseus' men are turned into pigs?

> **GCSE vocabulary:** ἀεί, βάλλω, ἔδωκα (δίδωμι), εἶναι (εἰμί), εἰσάγω, ἐν, ἐξέρχομαι, ἐπεί, ἔπειτα, ἕπομαι, ἔρχομαι, ἐρῶ (λέγω), ἔχω, ἦν (εἰμί), θύρα, ἵνα, καί, καλέω, κατά (+ acc.), κεφαλή, μέν ... δέ, ναῦς, οἶνος, πᾶς, πίνω, σῖτος, τε ... καί, φωνή, ὡς.

28 ἡ δ' – and she (*marking change of subject to Circe*); αἶψ' (= αἶψα, *see* Elision, *p.58*) – immediately; οἴγνυμι (*aorist* ὤϊξα) – open; φαεινός -ή -όν – gleaming.
29 κάλει (= ἐκάλει: *see* Missing augments, *p.58*; *compare also* ἕποντο) – '(she) was inviting them in'; ἅμα – at the same time; ἀϊδρείῃσιν (= ἀϊδρείαις: *see* Homeric grammatical forms, *p.59*) – 'in ignorance' (*a poetic plural*).
30 ὑπομένω (> μένω) – stay behind; οἴομαι (*aorist participle* ὀϊσάμενος) – think, suspect; δόλος ὁ – trick.
31 ἕζω (*aorist* εἶσα) – seat, sit down: *Circe is the subject of* εἷσεν *even though the change of subject is not made clear: supply 'them' (the men apart from Eurylochus) as the object;* κατά + *acc.* – down on; κλισμός ὁ (< recline) – couch; τε ... τε – both ... and; θρόνος ὁ (< throne) – seat, chair.
32 σφιν = αὐτοῖς; τυρός ὁ – cheese; ἄλφιτον τό – a barley grain; μέλι μέλιτος τό (< Melissa) – honey; χλωρός -ή -όν (< chlorine) – pale.
33 κυκάω – stir X (*acc.*) into Y (*dat.*); ἀναμίσγω – mix X (*acc.*) into Y (*dat.*).
34 φάρμακον – drug; λυγρός -ή -όν ruinous, baneful; πάγχυ (> πᾶς) – altogether; λανθάνομαι (*3rd plur. aorist optative* λαθοίατο) + *gen.* – forget; πατρίς -ίδος (> πατήρ) – of one's fathers (*fem. adjective*); αἶη ἡ – land.
35 αὐτάρ – *see l.1: here it marks a development in the narrative;* δῶκέν = ἔδωκε; ἐκπίνω (> πίνω) – drink up, drain; αὐτίκ' (= αὐτίκα) – at once.
36 ῥάβδος ἡ – stick; πεπληγυῖα – having struck (*fem. perf. participle act. of* πλήσσω); κατά ... ἐέργνυ (*by* Tmesis, *p.59*) *from* κατείργνυμι (*3rd sing. impf.* κατεέργνυ) – shut up, pen; συφεός ὁ – pigsty (συφεοῖσιν = συφεοῖς).
37 σῦς συός ὁ – pig; μέν – *here the contrast is expressed by* αὐτάρ (*l.38*), *rather than* δέ; ἔχον = εἶχον (*omitted augment*); τε ... τε ... – *these connect the two nouns which are accusatives of respect dependent on* κεφαλάς: 'the heads of pigs, with their grunts (*lit.* voice) and bristles'; θρίξ τριχός ἡ (< trichologist) – hair, bristle.
38 δέμας τό – body; αὐτάρ – *see l.1;* νοῦς ὁ – mind; ἔμπεδος -ον – unimpaired; τὸ πάρος – previously, before; πέρ – *this particle intensifies the comparison in* ὡς τὸ πάρος: *translate the whole phrase as* 'just as before'.
39 ὥς – *see l.16;* οἱ μέν – they (*the men apart from Eurylochus*); κλαίω – cry, weep; ἐέρχατο (*plup. pass. of* ἔργω) – (they) had been penned in; τοῖσι = αὐτοῖς.
40 πάρ ... ἔβαλεν *by tmesis from* παραβάλλω – throw down before; ῥ' (= ἄρα) – *see l.12;* ἄκυλος ἡ – acorn (*sing. for plur.*); βάλανος ἡ – mast (*fruit like acorns, eaten by pigs*); καρπός ὁ – fruit; κρανείη ἡ – cornel-tree (*a type of wild cherry*).
41 ἔδω (*present infinitive* ἔδμεναι) – eat; οἷα – 'such things as'; σῦς – *see l.37;* χαμαιευνάς -άδος – sleeping on the ground; αἰέν = ἀεί.
42 δ' (= δέ) – *contrasts with* μέν *in l.39;* ἄψ – back; θοός -ή -όν – swift; ἐπί + *acc.* – to, towards; νῆα = ναῦν; μέλας -αινα -αν (< melanoma) – black, dark.
43 ἀγγελίη ἡ – report, news; ἕταρος – *see l.23;* ἐρέων = ἐρῶν (*future participle of* λέγω *expressing purpose; see* Uncontracted forms, *p.59*); ἀδευκής -ές (ἀδευκέα *is the uncontracted masc. acc. sing.*) – bitter, dreadful; πότμος ὁ – fate.

Fifty lines are omitted from the set text in which Eurylochus in shock struggles to report what has happened, and then out of fear refuses to show Odysseus the way back to Circe's house. Odysseus, setting out on his own, encounters Hermes who promises to help by giving him a herb to counter Circe's drugs.

*Receiving the herb, Odysseus heads to Circe's house with some apprehension (*Odyssey *10. 302–19).*

ὣς ἄρα φωνήσας πόρε φάρμακον ἀργειφόντης
ἐκ γαίης ἐρύσας καί μοι φύσιν αὐτοῦ ἔδειξε.   45
ῥίζῃ μὲν μέλαν ἔσκε, γάλακτι δὲ εἴκελον ἄνθος·
μῶλυ δέ μιν καλέουσι θεοί· χαλεπὸν δέ τ' ὀρύσσειν
ἀνδράσι γε θνητοῖσι· θεοὶ δέ τε πάντα δύνανται.

  Ἑρμείας μὲν ἔπειτ' ἀπέβη πρὸς μακρὸν Ὄλυμπον
νῆσον ἀν' ὑλήεσσαν, ἐγὼ δ' ἐς δώματα Κίρκης   50
ἤια· πολλὰ δέ μοι κραδίη πόρφυρε κιόντι.
ἔστην δ' εἰνὶ θύρῃσι θεᾶς καλλιπλοκάμοιο·
ἔνθα στὰς ἐβόησα, θεὰ δέ μευ ἔκλυεν αὐδῆς.
ἡ δ' αἶψ' ἐξελθοῦσα θύρας ὤϊξε φαεινὰς
καὶ κάλει· αὐτὰρ ἐγὼν ἑπόμην ἀκαχήμενος ἦτορ.   55
εἷσε δέ μ' εἰσαγαγοῦσα ἐπὶ θρόνου ἀργυροήλου,
καλοῦ δαιδαλέου· ὑπὸ δὲ θρῆνυς ποσὶν ἦεν·
τεῦχε δέ μοι κυκεῶ χρυσέῳ δέπα, ὄφρα πίοιμι,
ἐν δέ τε φάρμακον ἧκε, κακὰ φρονέουσ' ἐνὶ θυμῷ.
αὐτὰρ ἐπεὶ δῶκέν τε καὶ ἔκπιον οὐδέ μ' ἔθελξε,   60
ῥάβδῳ πεπληγυῖα ἔπος τ' ἔφατ' ἔκ τ' ὀνόμαζεν·

Names
Ἑρμείας -αο ὁ: Hermes, *the messenger god.*

Ὄλυμπος -ου ὁ: Olympus, *a mountain in Thessaly where the gods were thought to live.*

Divine help
Gods regularly give mortals help in the *Odyssey*, as Hermes does here, although it is usually Athena who is the helper: she regularly assists Telemachus at the start of the poem as he seeks his father, she often comforts Penelope in Odysseus' absence, and she repeatedly helps Odysseus himself in his revenge against the suitors in the second half of the poem. However, this does not diminish the achievements of the heroes in ancient eyes, rather divine favour means success, and enhances the standing of the mortals whom they assist. The plant, moly, which Hermes here gives Odysseus to protect him from Circe's magic. is probably imaginary but, as Stanford observes, its description resembles black garlic, which was widely used in antiquity as a protective charm.

Repeated lines and scenes
Just as the poet repeatedly uses the same epithets to describe objects and people, he also repeats formulaic sections of lines (such as in line 61), whole lines, or even scenes. This can again help the poet in the act of oral composition, and his audience in following the story. However, the near repetition of scenes, such as we have with Circe's 'welcoming' of his men, and then Odysseus himself, can draw attention to significant aspects of the narrative.

> **GCSE vocabulary:** ἄγω (εἰσάγω), ἀνήρ, ἀποβαίνω, αὐτόν, βοάω, γε, ἐγώ, ἔδωκα (δίδωμι), εἰμί, εἰσάγω, ἐκ, ἐξέρχομαι, ἐπεί, ἔπειτα, ἕπομαι, ἤν (εἰμί), θεά, θεός, θύρα, καί, καλέω, κακός, καλός, με (ἐγώ), μέν ... δέ, μοι (ἐγώ), νῆσος, πᾶς, πίνω, πολύς, πούς, πρός, τε ... καί, φημί, χαλεπός.

44 ὥς – see l.16; ἄρα – see l.12; φωνέω – speak; πόρε (= ἐπόρε: see Missing augments, p.58) – '(he) gave'; φάρμακον – drug; ἀργειφόντης – Argos-slayer, *a common epithet of Hermes (Argos was a hundred-eyed giant, killed by him).*

45 γαίη ἡ – earth, ground; ἐρύω – pull up; φύσις -εως ἡ (< physics) – nature, quality; αὐτοῦ – *refers to the herb*; δείκνυμι (aor. ἔδειξα) – show.

46 ῥίζη ἡ – root; μέλας – black, dark; ἔσκον – *a Homeric imperfect of* εἰμί (I am); γάλα -ακτος τό (< galaxy) – milk; εἴκελος + dat. – like; ἄνθος τό (< chrysanthemum) – flower (*acc. of respect: translate as* 'in its flower').

47 μῶλυ τό – moly (*see the paragraph opposite on Divine help*); μιν = αὐτό; καλέουσι = καλοῦσι (see Uncontracted forms, p.59); τ' (= τε, see Elision, p.58) – *on its use, see l.15*; χαλεπόν – *supply* ἐστί *with this adjective*; ὀρύσσω – dig up.

48 θνητός -ή -όν – mortal; τε – see l.47; δύναμαι (< dynamic) – be capable of.

49 μακρός -ή -όν (< macrocosm) – long, high (*here*).

50 ἀν' (= ἀνά) + acc. – up over; ὑλήεις -εσσα -εν (> ὕλη) – wooded; ἐς = εἰς; δῶμα – house.

51 ἤϊα = ᾖα, *imperfect of* εἶμι (I go); πολλά (*adverbial*) – greatly (*here*); κραδίη ἡ – heart; πορφύρω (*imperfect without augment*, πόρφυρον) – boil, seethe; κίω – go (κιόντι *agrees with* μοι: *translate* 'my heart, as I went').

52 ἵσταμαι (aorist ἔστην) – stand; εἰνί = ἐν; θύρῃσι = θύραις (see Homeric grammatical forms, p.59); καλλιπλόκαμος (-οιο = -ου) – of beautiful hair.

53 ἔνθα – there; στάς – *aorist participle of* ἵσταμαι (see l.52); μευ – μου; κλύω + gen. – hear; αὐδή ἡ – voice.

54 = l.28.

55 κάλει – see l.29; αὐτάρ – see l.1; ἐγών = ἐγώ; ἑπόμην = εἱπόμην (*omitted augment*); ἀκαχήμενος -η -ον – afflicted, grieving; ἦτορ τό – heart (*accusative of respect:* 'in my heart').

56 ἕζω and θρόνος – see l.31; ἐπί + gen. – on; ἀργυρόηλος -ον – silver-studded.

57 δαιδαλέος -η -ον – skilfully-wrought; ὑπό ... ἦεν (3rd sing. impf., by Tmesis p.59, from ὕπειμι + dat.) – be under; θρῆνυς ὁ – stool; ποσίν = πουσίν.

58 τεύχω (τεῦχε = ἔτευχε) – prepare; κυκεών ὁ (acc. κυκεῶ) – mixed drink (*compare the one Circe made in lines 32–3*); χρύσεος -η -ον (> χρυσός) – golden; δέπας τό (dat. δέπα) – cup; ὄφρα = ἵνα, *introducing a purpose clause*.

59 ἐν ... ἧκε (3rd sing. aorist, by tmesis, from ἐνίημι) – put in; τε – *reinforces the connection of* δέ, *untranslatable*; φάρμακον – see l.44; φρονέω (*uncontracted*) – think; ἐνί = ἐν; θυμός – heart.

60 δῶκεν = ἔδωκεν; ἐκπίνω – drink up, drain; οὐδέ – see l.12; θέλγω – enchant.

61 ῥάβδῳ πεπληγυῖα – see l.36; ἔπος τό – word, speech; τε (*both times*) – and; ἔφατο = ἔφη; ἔκ ... ὀνόμαζεν (3rd sing. impf., by tmesis, from ἐξονομάζω) – utter aloud: *the second half of this line is a common formula introducing a speech*.

> Q. What is the effect on the narrative of the similarities and differences between this scene and the one in which Circe received Odysseus' men?
>
> Q. What is the effect of the narrative being told in the first person?

After Circe's magic fails, she is surprised but suggests love-making instead (Odyssey 10. 320–35).

'ἔρχεο νῦν συφεόνδε, μετ' ἄλλων λέξο ἑταίρων.'
ὣς φάτ', ἐγὼ δ' ἄορ ὀξὺ ἐρυσσάμενος παρὰ μηροῦ
Κίρκῃ ἐπήϊξα ὥς τε κτάμεναι μενεαίνων.
ἡ δὲ μέγα ἰάχουσα ὑπέδραμε καὶ λάβε γούνων,   65
καί μ' ὀλοφυρομένη ἔπεα πτερόεντα προσηύδα·

   'τίς πόθεν εἰς ἀνδρῶν; πόθι τοι πόλις ἠδὲ τοκῆες;
θαῦμά μ' ἔχει, ὡς οὔ τι πιὼν τάδε φάρμακ' ἐθέλχθης.
οὐδὲ γὰρ οὐδέ τις ἄλλος ἀνὴρ τάδε φάρμακ' ἀνέτλη,
ὅς κε πίῃ καὶ πρῶτον ἀμείψεται ἕρκος ὀδόντων.   70
σοὶ δέ τις ἐν στήθεσσιν ἀκήλητος νόος ἐστίν.
ἦ σύ γ' Ὀδυσσεύς ἐσσι πολύτροπος, ὅν τέ μοι αἰεὶ
φάσκεν ἐλεύσεσθαι χρυσόρραπις ἀργειφόντης,
ἐκ Τροίης ἀνιόντα θοῇ σὺν νηῒ μελαίνῃ.
ἀλλ' ἄγε δὴ κολεῷ μὲν ἄορ θέο, νῶϊ δ' ἔπειτα   75
εὐνῆς ἡμετέρης ἐπιβήομεν, ὄφρα μιγέντε
εὐνῇ καὶ φιλότητι πεποίθομεν ἀλλήλοισιν.'

Names

Ὀδυσσεύς -ῆος (*or* **-έος**) **ὁ**: Odysseus

Τροίη -ης ἡ: Troy

Supplication

When Odysseus charges at Circe with his sword as if to kill her, and she grabs his knees, this is the normal action of someone appealing to another in supplication. Odysseus himself, for example, is described as doing the same in book 7 when he appeals to Arete, the queen of the Phaeacians, to give him help to return to Ithaca.

> Q. How does Homer convey the swift change in the dynamics of the scene in lines 61–6?
>
> Q. What is the significance of the fact that Circe describes (in lines 72–4) how she has previously been told by Hermes of Odysseus' arrival?
>
> Q. How does this speech, if at all, change the impression we have of Circe?

> **GCSE vocabulary:** ἄγω, ἀεί, ἀλλά, ἄλλος, ἀνήρ, γάρ, γε, δή, ἐγώ, εἰμί, ἐκ, ἐν, ἔπειτα, ἔρχομαι, ἔχω, ἡμέτερος, καί, λαμβάνω, με (ἐγώ), μέγας, μέν... δέ, μετά (+ gen.), ναῦς, νῦν, ὅδε, ὅς, οὐ, παρά (+ gen.), πίνω, πόθεν, πόλις, πρῶτος, σύ, τίς, τις, φημί, ὡς.

62 ἔρχεο = ἔρχου (*imperative: see* Uncontracted forms, *p.59*); συφεόνδε (συφεός + δε: *a suffix meaning* 'towards') – to the pig sty; λέξο (*2nd sing. aor. imperative*) – 'lie down'; ἑταῖρος – *see l.1*.

63 ὥς – *see l.16*; φάτ' = ἔφατο (*see* Elision and Missing augments, *p.58*), *see l.61*; ἄορ τό – sword; ὀξύς -εῖα -ύ (< oxymoron) – sharp; ἐρύομαι (*aorist* εἰρυσσάμην) – draw; παρά + gen. – from beside; μηρός ὁ – thigh.

64 ἐπαίσσω (*aorist* ἐπήϊξα) + *dat.* – rush at; τε – *untranslatable: it emphasises the* ὡς 'just as (if)'; κτάμεναι = (ἀπο)κτείνειν; μενεαίνω – eagerly desire.

65 μέγα (*adverbial*) – loudly; ἰάχω – cry out; ὑποτρέχω – run up and under (the sword); λαμβάνω + gen. – grab hold of (*note omission of augment in* λάβε); γόνυ τό (*gen. plur.* γούνων) – knee.

66 ὀλοφύρομαι – wail, lament; ἔπεα – *uncontracted acc. plur. of* ἔπος, *see l.61*; πτερόεις -εσσα -εν – winged; προσαυδάω + *two accusatives* – address.

67 εἰς = εἶ 'you are'; ἀνδρῶν (*partitive genitive with* πόθεν) – 'among men'; πόθι = ποῦ; τοι = σοι (*possessive*); ἠδέ – and; τοκεύς ὁ (*nom. plur.* τοκῆες) – parent (*supply* εἰσί *with the two subjects*, πόλις *and* τοκῆες).

68 θαῦμα τό – wonder; ὡς – because, that; οὔ τι – not at all; φάρμακον – drug; ἐθέλχθης (*2nd sing. aorist passive of* θέλγω) – *see l.60*.

69 οὐδὲ γὰρ οὐδέ – for by no means; ἀνέτλην (*aorist: the verb has no present form*) – withstood.

70 ὅς κε πίῃ – 'whoever drinks' (κέ/ἄν + *subjunctive* = *indefinite construction*); ἀμείβομαι – pass (*supply* φάρμακα *as subject*; ἀμείψεται *is 3rd sing. aor. subj.*); ἕρκος -εος τό – barrier (*supply* 'whoever's' *here*); ὀδούς -όντος ὁ – tooth.

71 στῆθος -εος τό (< stethoscope) – breast (*poetic plural*); ἀκήλητος -η -ον – proof against magic; νόος ὁ – purpose.

72 ἦ – certainly; ἐσσι = εἶ; πολύτροπος -ον (> πολύς) – resourceful (*see* Homeric epithets, *p.62*); τε – *an untranslatable epic use of the particle, linking the additional information of the relative clause to the main clause*; αἰεί = ἀεί.

73 φάσκεν – *form of* ἔφη *used for repeated occurrences*; ἐλεύσεσθαι – *future infinitive of* ἔρχομαι (*indirect statement, with* ὅν *as subject of the infinitive*); χρυσόρραπις (> χρυσός) – with a golden wand; ἀργειφόντης – *see l.44*.

74 ἀνέρχομαι – I return; θοός – swift; σύν + *dat.* – with; μέλας – black, dark.

75 ἄγε – come on!; κολεόν τό – sheath; ἄορ – *see l.63*; τίθημι (θέο, *2nd sing. aor. imperative mid.*) – put; νῶϊ – the two of us (*nom. dual, see* Homeric grammatical forms, *p.59*).

76 εὐνή ἡ – bed, sex; ἐπιβήομεν + *gen.* – 'let us go to' (*1st plur. aor. subj. of* ἐπιβαίνω – mount, climb into, *a jussive subjunctive*); ὄφρα = ἵνα (*see l.58*); μίγνυμι (μιγέντε, *nom. dual of the aor. participle*) – I mix, engage in.

77 φιλότης -τητος ἡ – love-making; πεποίθομεν + *dat.* – *1st plur. perfect subjunctive of* πείθομαι; ἀλλήλους – each other (ἀλλήλοισιν = ἀλλήλοις).

Odysseus refuses until Circe swears an oath to do no more harm (Odyssey 10. 336–47).

ὣς ἔφατ', αὐτὰρ ἐγώ μιν ἀμειβόμενος προσέειπον·
'ὦ Κίρκη, πῶς γάρ με κέλεαι σοὶ ἤπιον εἶναι;
ἥ μοι σῦς μὲν ἔθηκας ἐνὶ μεγάροισιν ἑταίρους,   80
αὐτὸν δ' ἐνθάδ' ἔχουσα δολοφρονέουσα κελεύεις
ἐς θάλαμόν τ' ἰέναι καὶ σῆς ἐπιβήμεναι εὐνῆς,
ὄφρα με γυμνωθέντα κακὸν καὶ ἀνήνορα θήῃς.
οὐδ' ἂν ἐγώ γ' ἐθέλοιμι τεῆς ἐπιβήμεναι εὐνῆς,
εἰ μή μοι τλαίης γε, θεά, μέγαν ὅρκον ὀμόσσαι   85
μή τί μοι αὐτῷ πῆμα κακὸν βουλευσέμεν ἄλλο.'
   ὣς ἐφάμην, ἡ δ' αὐτίκ' ἀπόμνυεν, ὡς ἐκέλευον.
αὐτὰρ ἐπεί ῥ' ὄμοσέν τε τελεύτησέν τε τὸν ὅρκον,
καὶ τότ' ἐγὼ Κίρκης ἐπέβην περικαλλέος εὐνῆς.

23 lines are omitted from the set text, in which Circe's servants prepare a meal for Odysseus and bathe him. He is reluctant to eat (Odyssey 10. 371–4).

σῖτον δ' αἰδοίη ταμίη παρέθηκε φέρουσα,   90
εἴδατα πόλλ' ἐπιθεῖσα, χαριζομένη παρεόντων·
ἐσθέμεναι δ' ἐκέλευεν· ἐμῷ δ' οὐχ ἥνδανε θυμῷ,
ἀλλ' ἥμην ἀλλοφρονέων, κακὰ δ' ὄσσετο θυμός.

Direct speech
Two-thirds of the *Odyssey* is direct speech, a strikingly high proportion of the epic. On one level this makes the poem often resemble drama, where the characters are made to voice their thoughts and feelings directly to the listener, just as here Odysseus reveals his continuing fears and doubts to Circe by refusing to go at once to bed with her. However, on a larger scale, the narrative of books 9–12 is entirely narrated by Odysseus to an eager audience of Phaeacians on Scherie. This allows Homer to distance the 'monsters and marvels' of these books from his own narrative voice but, perhaps even more importantly, it gives a more personal voice to the account by the frequent use of the first person as in lines 90–4 here.

Q. What is the tone of Odysseus' speech to Circe here?

Q. Is it surprising that he agrees to go to bed with Circe while his companions are still pigs?

Q. How does Homer contrast the generous hospitality of the housekeeper with Odysseus' mood?

> **GCSE vocabulary:** ἀλλά, ἄλλος, αὐτός, γάρ, γε, ἐγώ, ἐθέλω, εἰ, εἶναι (εἰμί), ἐμός, ἐνθάδε, ἐπεί, ἔχω, θεά, ἰέναι (εἶμι), καί, κακός, κελεύω, λέγω, με (ἐγώ), μέγας, μέν… δέ, μή, μοι (ἐγώ), ὅς, πάρειμι, πολύς, πῶς, σῖτος, σύ, τε… καί, τις, τότε, φέρω, φημί, ὦ, ὡς

78 ὣς ἔφατ' – see l.63; αὐτάρ – see l.1; μιν = αὐτήν; ἀμείβομαι – answer; προσέειπον = προσεῖπον – 'I addressed'.
79 γάρ – 'No, for …'; κέλομαι – urge, order (κέλεαι = κέλῃ, see Homeric grammatical forms, p.59); ἤπιος -η -ον – gentle, kind.
80 ἥ – *a connecting relative, marking Circe as the subject*: 'you who'; σῦς – pigs (*acc. plur., see l.37*); ἔθηκας (*2nd sing. aor. act. of* τίθημι) – turn into (*here*); ἐνί = ἐν; μέγαρον τό (> μέγας) – hall (μεγάροισιν = μεγάροις); ἑταῖρος – see l.1.
81 αὐτόν – supply με *in agreement*; δολοφρονέων -ουσα -ον – cunning-minded.
82 ἐς = εἰς; θάλαμος ὁ – bedroom; ἐπιβήμεναι (*aor. inf. of* ἐπιβαίνω) – see l.76; εὐνή – see l.76.
83 ὄφρα = ἵνα (*see l.58*); γυμνόομαι – strip; κακός – cowardly, feeble (*here*); ἀνήνωρ -ορος (> ἀνήρ) – unmanly; θήῃς (*2nd sing. aor. subj. act. of* τίθημι) – see l.80.
84 οὐδέ – see l.12; ἄν + optative – would; τεός -ή -όν – your.
85 τλαίης (*2nd sing. aor. optative act. of* τλάω, *a form never found in the present*) – 'you were to be ready to'; ὅρκος ὁ – oath; ὄμνυμι + *future inf.* – swear (ὀμόσσαι *is aor. inf. act.*).
86 τί = τι (*accent thrown back from enclitic* μοι); πῆμα τό – suffering, harm; βουλεύω – devise (βουλευσέμεν = βουλεύσειν).
87 ὣς ἐφάμην – *first singular version of formula at l.63*; αὐτίκα – at once; ἀπόμνυμι – swear not to (ἀπώμνυον *is imperfect, see* Missing augments, p.58).
88 αὐτάρ – see l.1; ῥ' – see ll.12 and 40; ὄμοσα (*aor. of* ὄμνυμι) – see l.85; τε … τε – both … and; τελευτάω – complete (*the aorist here is missing the augment*); τόν = τοῦτον (*see* Uses of the article, p.58); ὅρκος – see l.85.
89 καί (*here emphasises* τότε) – indeed; ἐπιβαίνω – see l.76; περικαλλής -ές (> καλός) – very beautiful; εὐνή – see l.76.

90 σῖτος ὁ - bread (*here*); αἰδοῖος -η -ον – esteemed; ταμίη ἡ – housekeeper; παρατίθημι (*aorist* παρέθηκα) – place beside.
91 εἶδαρ -ατος τό – delicacy; ἐπιτίθημι (*aor. participle* ἐπιθείς) – put before, serve; χαρίζομαι – gratify, give freely of; παρεόντων (= παρόντων) – 'the things in store'.
92 ἐσθέμεναι = ἐσθίειν; ἁνδάνει + dat. – it pleases (*the imperfect here is missing the augment*); θυμός – see l.15.
93 ἧμαι (*imperfect* ἥμην) – sit; ἀλλοφρονέω (> ἄλλος) – think other thoughts; ὄσσομαι – have forebodings (*the imperfect here is missing the augment*).

*Odysseus is unmoved by Circe's reassurance but demands that she turn his companions back into human form (*Odyssey* 10. 375–87).*

Κίρκη δ' ὡς ἐνόησεν ἔμ' ἥμενον οὐδ' ἐπὶ σίτῳ
χεῖρας ἰάλλοντα, κρατερὸν δέ με πένθος ἔχοντα,   95
ἄγχι παρισταμένη ἔπεα πτερόεντα προσηύδα·
  'τίφθ' οὕτως, Ὀδυσεῦ, κατ' ἄρ' ἕζεαι ἶσος ἀναύδῳ,
θυμὸν ἔδων, βρώμης δ' οὐχ ἅπτεαι οὐδὲ ποτῆτος;
ἦ τινά που δόλον ἄλλον ὀΐεαι· οὐδέ τί σε χρὴ
δειδίμεν· ἤδη γάρ τοι ἀπώμοσα καρτερὸν ὅρκον.'   100
  ὣς ἔφατ', αὐτὰρ ἐγώ μιν ἀμειβόμενος προσέειπον·
'ὦ Κίρκη, τίς γάρ κεν ἀνήρ, ὃς ἐναίσιμος εἴη,
πρὶν τλαίη πάσσασθαι ἐδητύος ἠδὲ ποτῆτος,
πρὶν λύσασθ' ἑτάρους καὶ ἐν ὀφθαλμοῖσιν ἰδέσθαι;
ἀλλ' εἰ δὴ πρόφρασσα πιεῖν φαγέμεν τε κελεύεις,   105
λῦσον, ἵν' ὀφθαλμοῖσιν ἴδω ἐρίηρας ἑταίρους.'

Name
Ὀδυσεῦ: *vocative of* Odysseus. *(Note the name can be spelled with a single sigma as a metrically convenient alternative.)*

Food and drink
It was a normal part of hospitality for the Greeks to offer a guest food and drink although, of course, in this instance it only follows Circe's perverted hospitality in giving Odysseus' men drugged food to turn them into pigs, and her attempt to do the same to Odysseus himself. However, the change of Circe's approach is highlighted by the long description of the preparation of the meal in the omitted lines preceding line 90 of the set text. This extended passage also serves to create suspense for Odysseus' eventual refusal of the food, a mark of his great distress at the metamorphosis of his men. One may compare Priam's initial reluctance to eat in *Iliad* 24 following the death of Hector, until he is persuaded to by Achilles.

Q. How does it affect the narrative that we see Odysseus' grief through the eyes of Circe here?

Q. Is it significant that Circe does not realise the reason why Odysseus is still so upset? What does it say about her?

Q. Does the fact that Odysseus is the narrator affect the way we understand his speech in lines 102–6?

> **GCSE vocabulary:** ἀλλά, ἄλλος, ἀνήρ, γάρ, δή, ἐγώ, εἰ, εἴη (εἰμί), ἐν, ἔφαγον (ἐσθίω), ἔχω, ἤδη, ἴδω (ὁράω), ἵνα, καί, κελεύω, λέγω, λύω, ὅς, οὕτως, οὐχ, πίνω, σῖτος, σύ, τις, τίς, φημί, χείρ, χρή, ὦ, ὡς

94 νοέω – perceive, notice; ἧμαι (*participle* ἥμενος) – sit; οὐδέ – *see l.12*; ἐπί + *dat.* – at, to.
95 ἰάλλω – reach out; κρατερός -ή -όν – strong, violent; πένθος τό – grief.
96 ἄγχι – near; παρίσταμαι (*participle* παριστάμενος) – stand (beside); ἔπεα πτερόεντα προσηύδα – *see l.66*.
97 τίφθ' = τίπτε (*see* Elision, *p.58*) = τί ποτε – why ever?; κατ'... ἕζεαι *(by* Tmesis *p.59*, 2nd sing. from καθέζομαι, see Homeric grammatical forms, *p.59*) – sit; ἄρα – *see l.12*; ἴσος -η -ον + *dat.* (< isosceles) – equal, like; ἄναυδος -ον – speechless, mute.
98 θυμός – heart; ἔδω – eat, devour; βρώμη ἡ – food; ἅπτεαι (= ἅπτῃ) + *gen.* – touch; οὐδέ – *see l.12*; ποτής -ῆτος ἡ – drink.
99 ἦ – certainly; που – I suppose, doubtless; δόλος ὁ – trick; ὄϊεαι (= οἴῃ, 2nd sing. from οἴομαι) – think, suspect; τί = τι, *see l.86*.
100 δείδω (*infinitive* δειδίμεν) – fear; τοι = σοι; ἀπώμοσα (*aorist of* ἀπόμνυμι) – *see l.87*; καρτερός – *see l.95*; ὅρκος – oath.
101 *See l.78.*
102 γάρ – *explaining why he is not eating: translate* 'no, for ...'; κεν – would (*with the optative verb* τλαίη *in l.102*); ὅς – whoever (*introducing the indefinite construction in historic sequence with the optative* εἴη); ἐναίσιμος -ον – decent, fair.
103 πρίν – previously, sooner (*adverb, anticipating the second* πρίν *in line 104*); τλαίη – *3rd sing., see l.85*; πατέομαι (*aorist* ἐπασσάμην) + *gen.* – eat, consume; ἐδητύς -ύος ἡ – food; ἠδέ – and; ποτής – *see l.98*.
104 πρίν + *infinitive* – before; λύομαι – get X freed; ἕταρος = ἑταῖρος, *see l.1*; ἐν + *dat.* – with (*here*); ὀφθαλμός ὁ – eye; ἰδέσθαι – *aor. inf. mid. of* ὁράω: *translate like the active* ἰδεῖν.
105 πρόφρασσα (*feminine adjective*) – kindly; φαγέμεν = φαγεῖν (*see* Homeric grammatical forms, *p.59*); τε – and (*see l.23*).
106 ὀφθαλμός – *see l.104*; ἐρίηρος (*acc. plur.* -ας) – trusty; ἑταῖρος – *see l.1*.

Circe agrees to Odysseus' request, and there is an emotional reunion between Odysseus and his men (Odyssey 10. 388–99).

ὣς ἐφάμην, Κίρκη δὲ διὲκ μεγάροιο βεβήκει
ῥάβδον ἔχουσ' ἐν χειρί, θύρας δ' ἀνέῳξε συφειοῦ,
ἐκ δ' ἔλασεν σιάλοισιν ἐοικότας ἐννεώροισιν.
οἱ μὲν ἔπειτ' ἔστησαν ἐναντίοι, ἡ δὲ δι' αὐτῶν   110
ἐρχομένη προσάλειφεν ἑκάστῳ φάρμακον ἄλλο.
τῶν δ' ἐκ μὲν μελέων τρίχες ἔρρεον, ἃς πρὶν ἔφυσε
φάρμακον οὐλόμενον, τό σφιν πόρε πότνια Κίρκη·
ἄνδρες δ' ἂψ ἐγένοντο νεώτεροι ἢ πάρος ἦσαν
καὶ πολὺ καλλίονες καὶ μείζονες εἰσοράασθαι.   115
ἔγνωσαν δ' ἐμὲ κεῖνοι, ἔφυν τ' ἐν χερσὶν ἕκαστος·
πᾶσιν δ' ἱμερόεις ὑπέδυ γόος, ἀμφὶ δὲ δῶμα
σμερδαλέον κονάβιζε· θεὰ δ' ἐλέαιρε καὶ αὐτή.

Crying

Here Odysseus and his men cry tears of joy at the way they are reunited, but tears are a common feature of the *Odyssey* and the hero himself often cries, most notably perhaps in book 8, when he listens to the songs of the Phaeacian bard Demodocus about episodes from the Trojan War. After the last such song, about the fall of Troy, Odysseus is said to have wept like a woman over her husband who has died in battle. Greek heroes displayed their emotions.

Figure 8 *Odysseus rushes at Circe with a sword – she is in flight and dropping her cup. Red-figure terracotta calyx-krater, Greek, Attic, c. 440 BCE. How similar is this portrayal of Odysseus' attack upon Circe to that in Homer's narrative?*
Photo: Metropolitan Museum of Art, 41.83, Gift of Amelia E. White, 1941.

GCSE vocabulary: ἄλλος, ἀνήρ, αὐτός, βαίνω, γίγνομαι, γιγνώσκω, διά (+ gen.), ἐγώ, εἰμί, ἐκ, ἕκαστος, ἐκεῖνος, ἐλαύνω, ἐν, ἔπειτα, ἔρχομαι, ἔχω, ἤ, θεά, θύρα, καί, καλλίων (καλός), μείζων (μέγας), μέν … δέ, νέος, ὁράω, ὅς, πᾶς, πολύς, φημί, χείρ.

107 ὣς ἐφάμην – *see l.87*; διέκ + *gen.* – out through; μέγαρον – hall (μεγάροιο = μεγάρου, *see* Homeric grammatical forms, *p.59*); βεβήκει (*3rd sing. pluperfect of* βαίνω) – 'she had gone'.
108 ῥάβδος – stick; ἀνοίγνυμι (*aorist* ἀνέῳξα); συφειός (= συφεός) – pigsty.
109 ἐκ … ἔλασεν – *from* ἐξελαύνω (*by* Tmesis, *see p.59*); σίαλος ὁ – fat hog (σιάλοισιν = σιάλοις, *see* Homeric grammatical forms, *p.59*); ἐοικώς -ότος + *dat.* – resembling; ἐννέωρος -ον – nine-year-old.
110 ἵσταμαι (*aorist* ἔστην) – stand; ἐναντίος -η -ον – opposite, facing.
111 προσαλείφω – anoint, smear (προσάλειφεν *is imperfect, see* Missing augments, *p.58*); φάρμακον – drug.
112 τῶν = αὐτῶν (*see* Uses of the article, *p.58*); μέλος -εος τό – limb; θρίξ τρίχος – hair, bristle; ῥέω – fall off; πρίν – previously; φύω – produce, cause to grow.
113 οὐλόμενος -η -ον – accursed, deadly; τό = ὅ (*relative pronoun, see* Uses of the article, *p.58*); σφιν = αὐτοῖς; πόρω – provide, give (*the imperfect here is missing the augment*); πότνια – lady, queen (*female honorific epithet*).
114 ἄψ – back, again; πάρος – before, previously.
115 πολύ – much (*adverbial*); εἰσοράασθαι – 'to look at'.
116 κεῖνοι = ἐκεῖνοι (*see* Homeric grammatical forms, *p.59*); ἔφυν ἐν χερσίν – '(he) clasped by the hands'.
117 ἱμερόεις -εσσα -εν – pleasing, joyful; ὑποδύω (*3rd sing. aorist* ὑπέδυ) + *dat.* – come upon, come over; γόος ὁ – lamentation; ἀμφί + *acc.* – around; δῶμα – house.
118 σμερδαλέον (*adverbial*) – terribly; κονάβιζω – ring out (*note missing augment on this imperfect and the next*); ἐλεαίρω – pity, feel pity.

Q. What is the effect of calling Circe πότνια Κίρκη, when Odysseus reminds his audience of the first, harmful drug she had given his men?

Q. Why are we told that even Circe felt pity in the last line?

What happens next?

Odysseus fetches the other half of his crew and they feast at Circe's house for a whole year, until finally his men urge him that it is time to move on. Circe tells Odysseus that to find his way home he must go to the House of Hades to consult the spirit of the dead prophet Teiresias. Odysseus' visit to the Underworld is the story of the next book, before the final round of seafaring adventures in book 12, which includes the Sirens, the Cattle of the Sun, and two encounters with Scylla and Charybdis, the latter of whom destroys Odysseus' ship in her huge whirlpool, before he escapes shipwrecked onto Calypso's island.

This marks the end of Odysseus' narrative of his adventures in flashback, and the second half of the epic focuses on Odysseus' return to Ithaca, and the challenges which face him there. In his absence, a group of local nobles has begun competing to usurp his position as ruler by taking his place as the husband of Penelope. These suitors have been staying in his palace, consuming his possessions and have been pressuring Penelope, against her wishes, to take one of them as a new husband on the grounds that Odysseus will never return. Penelope, matching her husband's cunning and endurance, has delayed them by saying that she will choose one of them as soon as she has finished weaving a burial shroud for Odysseus' father, Laertes, only to unpick each day's work in secret at night.

Odysseus returns disguised (with Athene's help) as a beggar and is able to ascertain who in the palace remains loyal to him, before a final showdown with the suitors. After her ruse has been exposed, Penelope sets them the challenge of stringing Odysseus' bow and firing an arrow through a series of axe-heads lined up in the main hall of the palace to decide which of them she will marry. All the suitors who try fail, unable even to string the bow, but Odysseus, still disguised as a beggar, completes the challenge. At this point, Athene reveals him in his full glory and, together with his son and some loyal servants, he proceeds brutally to slaughter all the suitors who are trapped in the hall.

Penelope sets her husband a final test, as she initially refuses to believe that he really has returned. She gives an instruction that their bed be moved out of their bedchamber. When Odysseus objects, saying that this is impossible since it is built around the trunk of an olive tree, she relents and accepts that he is, indeed, her husband. They go to bed together and he recounts to her the tale of his exploits; the next day he makes peace with the families of the suitors that he has so violently killed.

Final questions

- How far does the Circe episode reflect Odysseus' famed qualities of cunning and endurance?
- How do the stories of Odysseus' adventures in the magic and miraculous world of the first half of the poem relate to the story of his return and revenge in the second half?
- This poem was composed over 2,500 years ago and was intended to be performed orally. Do you think it still works well for a modern reader?

Euripides

Euripides was one of the three most celebrated writers of tragedy in fifth-century Athens. We have eighteen complete plays out of the 90 or so that he wrote, as well as a range of fragments from some of his other plays. This is more than the combined total of Aeschylus and Sophocles, two other great playwrights of the period, from whose works seven plays each survive.

Very little hard evidence exists about Euripides' life. There are plenty of stories from ancient authors, but they seem to have been invented either from material in his own plays or from the portrayal of him in contemporary comedies like *Frogs* by Aristophanes. He was born *c.* 480 BCE and died *c.* 407/6 BCE. We have rather better information about the dates of his plays. Since these were written for a competition, each year records were kept of the title, author and place gained by the play. *Trojan Women* was first performed in 415 BCE, as part of a trilogy of tragedies; the trilogy was awarded second prize (out of three).

Drama in Ancient Greece

Drama is one of the great innovations to have come out of Ancient Greece. Classical drama continues to have a significant influence on modern theatre and many plays from Ancient Greece have been subject to revival over the past 100 years.

When we talk about Greek drama, we are really speaking of Athenian drama, for it was in Athens that the plays that we have were first written and performed. The rise of drama was closely tied up with the development of democracy, another great Athenian innovation. Although the content of the plays was based on mythology, the issues explored were frequently relevant to their time, and indeed continue to be so today. The fact that they were expressed as myth meant that issues could be explored in a safe environment without the passions that discussion in the Assembly, the democratic decision-making body of Athens, might provoke.

The presentation of drama was very different from our current practice. Plays are now put on typically for a run of several weeks or more; they are performed inside with artificial lighting, generally in the evening. Members of the audience come alone, in pairs, or perhaps as a group, with the aim of being entertained or perhaps to learn something. A large theatre today may seat an audience of about 1,000 people.

Greek drama took place in the context of a religious festival. The principal dramatic festival in Athens, the City Dionysia, took place in the spring once sea-travel had restarted after the winter, and lasted for the best part of a week, but preparations began long before. At the start of the festival there was a procession where tribute from the subject allies of Athens was paraded through the agora and into the theatre for citizens and visitors to see and admire. Bulls were sacrificed to Dionysus and wine (plenty of it) was drunk to honour him. On this opening day, group choral songs called *dithyrambs* were performed. These involved 1,000 ordinary Athenians, 500 men and 500 boys, arranged into groups of 50 by tribes (a somewhat artificial division of the citizen body into smaller units). For much of the period for which we have a record, the next days were filled with theatrical performances: in one day, five comedies were put on. On three other days, four plays by the same author were presented each day, three tragedies and a less-serious satyr play. At the end, judges, selected from the ten tribes by lot, awarded the prize for the best playwright. To the Greeks, competition (as was also demonstrated in their athletic festivals) was central to bringing out the best that men can produce to honour the gods.

The plays were written in verse, using a combination of long speeches, dialogue over alternate lines, and odes in a variety of lyric metres sung by the chorus and, occasionally, actors. There were three professional actors only, always men, who took on all the speaking roles. In addition to their costumes, they wore masks which helped to make their character clear from a distance. Apart from non-speaking extras, there were 15 other key participants – the chorus. Their training, as well as the other costs of production, were financed by a wealthy citizen in a form of taxation known as a *liturgy*. The chorus was recruited from ordinary Athenian male citizens who spent several months learning the words, music and dance that comprised the performance. The complexity of the choral rhythms meant that this would have been an intense period of hard work. Since many Athenians would have performed choral songs in the *dithyrambs*, the audience would have been knowledgeable and appreciative of this art.

The space for performances was an open-air site on the south side of the Acropolis which held around 15,000 spectators. Such a large gathering of citizens was inevitably treated as a significant civic event, an opportunity to celebrate both the unity of the city-state and the success of the democracy by which it was governed, as in the parade of tribute from subject allies mentioned above. The plays presented might celebrate Athens and its political system, but they might also ask difficult questions of the actions taken in Athens' name. *Trojan Women*, for example, is considered by some scholars to have been written with events the previous year on the island of Melos in mind. The island had abandoned its previous neutrality in the war between Athens and Sparta to show active support for the latter. Athens exacted brutal revenge for this, destroying the city, killing its male citizens and enslaving the city's women and children. Euripides' play presents the arrogance of Greek victors at Troy as they mercilessly destroy the city and treat its women and children with similar brutality: it also shows the audience that the victors' journey home will be fatal for many and that this is the punishment from the gods for their behaviour. All this may well have been uneasy viewing for the citizens of Athens in 415 BCE.

The theatre itself was part of a larger complex of the sanctuary of the god Dionysus after whom the festival was named (Dionysia). The spectators sat on the natural slope of the hill and had an open view of city and countryside beyond. A circular area of beaten earth called the *orchestra* (or 'area for dancing') formed the main performance area for the actors and the chorus. At the back of the *orchestra*, facing the audience, was a wooden stage building (σκηνή < scene) sitting on a raised wooden platform. This had a double door in the middle representing an interior space – typically the palace of the king – although it could indicate other settings such as a peasant cottage or a cave. There were also entrances (*parodoi*) from either side of the *orchestra*. Since the *orchestra* was about 24 metres in diameter, entrances and exits from the side to the centre would have taken the actors an appreciable amount of time.

If you have seen pictures of Greek theatres or have been lucky enough to visit one, it is worth bearing in mind that they may be of a later date. Over time, theatres became grander, with stone seating and a permanent *skene*. Remains of the Theatre of Dionysus survive in Athens, but what we see was modified by the Romans 500 years after plays like *Trojan Women* were originally performed.

Greek tragedy as poetry

Greek tragedy is written in verse which follows certain rhythmic patterns. The lines you will read are *iambic trimeters*, which usually have 12 syllables. There are a few noteworthy features of the text which are consequences of the poetic nature of the work:

1. If a word ends in a vowel and the following word begins with a vowel, the first word may drop its final vowel (elision) or it may join with the next word (crasis). If the next word begins with an aspirated vowel, and if the consonant exposed by the elided final vowel can aspirate, it will do so.

(NB crasis can easily be spotted because the second word keeps a mark that resembles a breathing over its initial vowel, even though the word formed by crasis may well now begin with a consonant.)

e.g.
line 1: θ' ἥσυχον = τε ἥσυχον (elision, *but the exposed* τ' *aspirates to* θ' *because the first letter of* ἥσυχον *is itself aspirated, i.e. has a rough breathing*).

line 4: ἐς στράτευμ' Ἀχαιϊκόν – ἐς στράτευμα Ἀχαιϊκόν (elision).

line 8: κεἰ = καί εἰ (crasis – *initial consonant, but the breathing of* εἰ *is apparently retained*).

2. Another feature of Greek tragedy is that, like all Classical poetry, the word order is a lot more flexible than its prose equivalent. This allows the poet to focus emphasis effectively, but it also means that, when translating, you will have to be even more careful to find the subject, verb and object of each phrase, and to apply each adjective to the correct noun.

3. An associated characteristic of Classical poetry, inherited from the Homeric poems, is omission of the article from its noun. Line 1, for example, contains four nouns and none of them have an article but they are translated as if they did (rather like a noun in Latin). This takes some getting used to because you have learned that the article is very helpful in establishing the case of a noun and thereby its function in a sentence. Where this causes particular difficulty, the notes offer assistance.

4. Finally, the poetic nature of Greek tragedy is sometimes reflected in the unusual, often archaic, poetic forms of some parts of nouns, pronouns and verbs. These are highlighted for you in the notes and the more familiar version of the form is indicated.

2027–28 Prescription

This selection corresponds to Euripides' Trojan Women *lines 654–78, and 686–779.*

The backstory

The war and siege of Troy lay at the heart of ancient Greek identity. Not only was the story viewed as historical fact, but also as a defining moment in which independent Greek city-states came together for a common cause, during which some of the greatest heroes of the past secured undying glory. Helen, wife of Menelaus, King of Sparta, was abducted to Troy by her lover, the Trojan prince, Paris. Menelaus and his brother, Agamemnon King of Mycenae, gathered an alliance of Greek states into an armada that sailed to sack Troy and restore Helen to her husband. Over the next ten years, great heroes from amongst both the Greeks and the Trojans, like Achilles and Hector, fought and died. With the death of Hector, immortalised in Homer's poem the *Iliad*, Troy's fate was sealed. Later, thinking the war was over and the Greeks had gone, the Trojans unwittingly brought Greek soldiers, hidden in a wooden horse, into the heart of their city. While Troy slept, the hidden soldiers, released by Helen, let their comrades in, the city was set on fire and carnage ensued: the Trojan king, Priam, was murdered at an altar of the gods, and Troy's fighting force was slaughtered. Euripides focuses his drama on the moment when resistance is over; the fires of the city burn in the background as Troy's women and children, gathered on the seashore, await distribution as booty of war to the Greek soldiers before they head back, victorious, to their homes. But Euripides' play is not at all a picture of Greek triumph, but of the brutal consequences for these women, helpless now that they have lost their city and their men to war.

Figure 9 *An image of the family of Hector, with Andromache and the young Astyanax, in happier times. The association of wife and child with Hector is precisely what secures their fate. Apulian red-figure column-krater, c. 370–360 BCE.*
Photo: Wikimedia Commons: Jastrow.

The play so far

The play opens with the gods Poseidon and Athena agreeing to punish the Greek victors at Troy for their impious behaviour in the ruins of the city by destroying them in a storm on their journey home. Knowledge of this overshadows everything that happens at the hands of the Greeks during the play. Hecuba, Priam's queen, is on stage, as she is throughout the play; a widowed royal wife, a mother and a grandmother, she is the medium through which Euripides explores both the suffering of the women of Troy and also their varied response to that suffering.

The chorus of Trojan women enter and, with Hecuba, lament the loss of their freedom and imminent allocation as slaves to different Greek warriors. The Greek herald, Talthybius, enters to announce some of those allocations; Hecuba's daughter, Cassandra, a priestess who can see the future, enters in marriage regalia. She has been allocated to the Greek commander-in-chief, Agamemnon, and foretells how, at the cost of her own life, she will bring about his death on his return home. Cassandra is led off.

Hecuba, devastated, collapses, only to be raised by the chorus to greet Andromache, her daughter-in-law. She is brought onstage in a cart along with her son, Astyanax, and the weapons of her dead husband, Hector. Andromache brings further dreadful news, the slaughter of another of Hecuba's daughters, Polyxena, who has been sacrificed to the spirit of Achilles at his tomb. Andromache considers Polyxena lucky; her troubles are now over, whereas her own have just begun and will only get worse. Hecuba is trying to reason with her when our extract begins.

Figure 10 *That innocent women and children are often the brutal victims of war, reflected in Euripides' play* The Trojan Women, *is made very clear in this depiction of the death of Astyanax on an Etruscan red-figure calyx krater attributed to the Nazzano Painter. From Civita Castellana, fourth century* BCE.
Photo by DEA / G. NIMATALLAH/De Agostini via Getty Images.

Andromache laments that her qualities as a wife have now made her more attractive to her enemies. She wonders how she should respond to her new male master (Trojan Women 654–66).

Andromache γλώσσης τε σιγὴν ὄμμα θ' ἥσυχον πόσει
παρεῖχον· ᾔδη δ' ἁμ' ἐχρῆν νικᾶν πόσιν
κείνῳ τε νίκην ὧν ἐχρῆν παριέναι.
καὶ τῶνδε κληδὼν ἐς στράτευμ' Ἀχαϊκὸν
ἐλθοῦσ' ἀπώλεσέν μ'· ἐπεὶ γὰρ ᾑρέθην, 5
Ἀχιλλέως με παῖς ἐβουλήθη λαβεῖν
δάμαρτα· δουλεύσω δ' ἐν αὐθεντῶν δόμοις.
κεἰ μὲν παρώσασ' Ἕκτορος φίλον κάρα
πρὸς τὸν παρόντα πόσιν ἀναπτύξω φρένα,
κακὴ φανοῦμαι τῷ θανόντι· τόνδε δ' αὖ 10
στυγοῦσ' ἐμαυτῆς δεσπόταις μισήσομαι.
καίτοι λέγουσιν ὡς μί' εὐφρόνη χαλᾷ
τὸ δυσμενὲς γυναικὸς εἰς ἀνδρὸς λέχος·

Names and places

Ἀχαϊκός -ή -όν: Greek. *Euripides imitates Homer by using several different words to refer to the Greeks and Trojans.*

Ἀχιλλεύς -έως ὁ: Achilles. *The greatest of the warrior heroes fighting with Agamemnon against Troy. He killed Hector and himself was slain before Troy fell. His son, Neoptolemus, has been allocated Andromache as his war prize to take back to Greece.*

Ἕκτωρ -ορος ὁ: Hector. *The greatest of Priam's sons and of the Trojan heroes. He was married to Andromache and killed by Achilles before Troy fell.*

Marriage, subservience and slavery

In her speech Andromache identifies the behaviour which marks her out as a good wife and which is the foundation of her fame: her qualities would also have been acknowledged by the, mostly male, fifth-century Athenian audience who, as Pericles made clear in his 'funeral speech' at Athens in 431 BCE, valued a wife who was quiet and obedient. Achilles' son, Neoptolemos, may indeed have been equally attracted by these qualities and have wanted to take Andromache as his 'wife', as she claims. But she also makes it clear that her relationship with Achilles's son will be very different: as a wife she retained a degree of independence and the capacity, in some areas of married life, to be master over her husband – just as an Athenian wife would manage domestic matters and the household slaves. With him, however, she will be enslaved, and her role will be little more than a sexual one.

> Q. What qualities of a wife does Andromache specifically highlight? Are you surprised by any of these?
>
> Q. What are the factors that contribute to the confusion Andromache feels about how to treat her new master?
>
> Q. What is the added horror for Andromache in being allocated as a slave to, of all people, the son of Achilles? How does this colour our response to her confusion here?

GCSE vocabulary: αἱρέω (ᾑρέθην), ἀνήρ, βούλομαι, γλῶσσα, γυνή, δέ, δεσπότης, ἐγώ, ἔρχομαι (ἐλθοῦσα), ἐπεί, εἰ, ἐν, καί, κακός, λαμβάνω, λέγω, μία (εἷς), μισέω (μισήσομαι), νικάω, νίκη, ὅδε, οἶδα (ᾔδη), παῖς, παρέχω (παρεῖχον), πρός, σιγή, φαίνομαι (φανοῦμαι), φίλος, χρή.

1 τε (*placed after the word it is translated in front of, often combined with another* τε – *here written as* θ' *aspirated and elided: see* elision, *p.81*) – 'both. . . and'; ὄμμα -ατος τό – eye; ἥσυχος -ον – silent (*a 'silent eye' is one that sees something but does not comment*); πόσις -εως ὁ – husband.

2 παρεῖχον (*1st sing. imperfect indicative of* παρέχω); ᾔδη – I knew (*1st sing. past tense of* οἶδα; *the objects of this verb are the two relative clauses* 'I knew the things in which. . . and the things which. . .'); δ' = δε; ἅμ' (= ἅ + ἐμέ: *see* crasis *and* elision, *p.81*) – 'the things in which I. . .' (ἅ *is an accusative of respect*, ἐμέ *is accusative following* χρή + *acc.*); πόσιν – *see l.1*.

3 = 'and the things in which I had to yield the victory to that man'; κείνῳ (= ἐκείνῳ) – *dative following* παριέναι; τε – and (*see l.1, here on its own linking the two relative clauses*); ὧν – the things which (*genitive with* νίκην); παριέναι (*present infinitive of* παρίημι) – to yield.

4 κληδών -όνος ἡ – report; στράτευμα -ατος τό – army.

5 ἐλθοῦσ' = ἐλθοῦσα; ἀπόλλυμι (*aorist* ἀπώλεσα) – destroy; μ' = με.

7 δάμαρ -αρτος ἡ – 'as his wife' (*in apposition to* με); δουλεύω – be a slave; αὐθέντης -ου ὁ – murderer; δόμος -ου ὁ – house (δόμοις, *plural for singular*).

8 κεἰ = καὶ εἰ (*see* crasis, *p.81*), *introducing a condition referring to the future* (ἀναπτύξω *l.9*); παρώσασ' = παρώσασα (*aorist participle, fem. nom. sing. of* παρωθέω, *aorist* παρέωσα) – rejecting; φίλον – (φίλος *as an adjective*) beloved; κάρα τό (= κεφαλή) *taken with* Ἕκτορος – 'the head of Hector', i.e. Hector.

9 πόσις – *see l.1*; ἀναπτύσσω (*future* ἀναπτύξω) – open up; φρήν -ενός ἡ (< phrenology) – heart, mind.

10 θανόντι (*from* θνήσκω > ἀποθνῄσκω) – die; δ'αὖ – but on the other hand.

11 στυγοῦσ' (= στυγοῦσα, *participle replacing conditional clause*) *from* στυγέω – hate; ἐμαυτῆς (*take with* δεσπόταις) – my own; μισέομαι (*future middle used as a future passive*, μισήσομαι) (< misanthrope) + *dat.* – I am hateful to.

12 καίτοι – and yet; ὡς = ὅτι; μί' = μία; εὐφρόνη -ης ἡ – night; χαλάω – loosen.

13 τὸ δυσμενές – hostility (*the neuter adjective with the article creates the abstract noun*); εἰς – towards (*here*); λέχος -ους τό – bed (*literally: but often refers to sex that will take place in the bed*).

Andromache continues to lament her husband and the imminent loss of her freedom. Her mother, Hecuba, queen of Troy, widow of Priam and mother to many children who have been killed in the war, is more pragmatic (Trojan Women 667–78; 686–9).

  ἀπέπτυσ' αὐτὴν ἥτις ἄνδρα τὸν πάρος
  καινοῖσι λέκτροις ἀποβαλοῦσ' ἄλλον φιλεῖ.   15
  ἀλλ' οὐδὲ πῶλος ἥτις ἂν διαζυγῇ
  τῆς συντραφείσης ῥαδίως ἕλξει ζυγόν.
  καίτοι τὸ θηριῶδες ἄφθογγόν τ' ἔφυ
  ξυνέσει τ' ἄχρηστον τῇ φύσει τε λείπεται.
  σὲ δ', ὦ φίλ' Ἕκτορ, εἶχον ἄνδρ' ἀρκοῦντά μοι   20
  ξυνέσει γένει πλούτῳ τε κἀνδρείᾳ μέγαν·
  ἀκήρατον δέ μ' ἐκ πατρὸς λαβὼν δόμων
  πρῶτος τὸ παρθένειον ἐζεύξω λέχος.
  καὶ νῦν ὄλωλας μὲν σύ, ναυσθλοῦμαι δ' ἐγὼ
  πρὸς Ἑλλάδ' αἰχμάλωτος ἐς δοῦλον ζυγόν.   25

In the omitted lines (679–85), Andromache compares her fate to that of her sister-in-law, Polyxena, slaughtered on the tomb of Achilles: Polyxena's suffering is finished, but Andromache is not even consoled by hope – only suffering lies ahead. The Chorus agree and liken her pain to their own.

Hecuba αὐτὴ μὲν οὔπω ναὸς εἰσέβην σκάφος,
    γραφῇ δ' ἰδοῦσα καὶ κλύουσ' ἐπίσταμαι.
    ναύταις γὰρ ἢν μὲν μέτριος ᾖ χειμὼν φέρειν,
    προθυμίαν ἔχουσι σωθῆναι πόνων,

Animals and humans

The relationship between ancient Greeks and domesticated animals – whether as an indication of status, or in working the land, as a means of transport, source of food, or part of religious ritual – was necessarily very close. This proximity prompted reflection upon the similarities between the behaviour of animals and humans, but therefore also on what distinguishes the two. Plato and others, like Andromache here, frame this distinction in terms of a human's unique powers of reason and of speech, implying superiority over an animal: despite this distinction, Andromache points out that even a brute animal feels the loss of its partner.

Athens and her fleet

The world of ships and sailing ran in the blood of the average Athenian; Athens' fleet was central to her power in the Greek world in the fifth century BCE. Not only had the fleet been at the heart of Greek resistance to the Persians in 480 BCE, but it had also enabled Athens to generate and police the empire that emerged after victory over the Persians. The free citizens of Athens, the audience in the theatre, were also the oarsmen in the triremes of her fleet. Nautical references, in metaphor and analogy, used by Hecuba, would have been appreciated and enjoyed by the audience.

> Q. How does Andromache's reference to a young horse in lines 16–21 resolve the dilemma of how a woman in her position should behave?
>
> Q. What different uses of the idea of a 'yoke' does Andromache employ?

GCSE vocabulary: αἰχμάλωτος, ἀλλά, ἄλλος, ἄν, ἀνήρ, αὐτός, δοῦλος, ἑαυτόν, ἐγώ, εἰμί, εἰσβαίνω (εἰσέβην), ἐπί, Ἑλλάς, ἔχω (εἶχον), ὁράω, καί, λαμβάνω, λείπω, μέγας, μέν. . .δέ. . ., ναῦς (ναός), ναύτης, νῦν, πατήρ, πρῶτος, πρός, ῥᾴδιος, σύ, σῴζω (σωθῆναι), φέρω, φιλέω, χειμών.

14 ἀπέπτυσ' (= ἀπέπτυσα: *this use of the aorist to express what Andromache wants to do now as if she has already done it, is colloquial and dramatic*) – spit out, loathe; ἥτις – *an alternative relative pronoun* (= ἥ, *fem. nom. sing.*); τὸν πάρος (*take with* ἄνδρα) – previous (husband).

15 καινός -ή -όν (καινοῖσι = καινοῖς, *see* poetic forms, *p.81*) – new; λέκτρον -ου τό (> λέχος *see l.13*) – bed (*plural for singular, dative of advantage: translate as* 'for the sake of a bed'); ἀποβαλοῦσ' = ἀποβαλοῦσα.

16 οὐδέ (> οὐ) – not even; πῶλος -ου ἡ – filly, young horse; ἥτις (*with* ἄν + *subjunctive: indefinite*) – which(ever); διαζυγῇ (*aorist subjunctive passive from* διαζεύγνυμι) + *gen.* – is separated (*lit.* 'unyoked') from.

17 τῆς συντραφείσης – workmate (*lit. the one she was reared with*); ἕλξει (*fut. of* ἕλκω) – pull at; ζυγόν -οῦ τό – yoke (*what joins one draft animal to another*).

18 καίτοι – and yet; τὸ θηριῶδες – a creature (*compare l.13, but in addition the article indicates this is a class or type*); ἄφθογγος -ον (< diphthong) – without speech; τ'. . .τ' (*see l.1: here they link the two adjectives* ἄφθογγον & ἄχρηστον) – both. . . and; ἔφυ (*from* φύω) (< physical) – be by nature.

19 ξυνέσις -εως ἡ – understanding; ἄχρηστος -ον – devoid of; φύσις -εως ἡ (> φύω *l.18*) – nature; τε – and (*see l.3: here it links the two verbs* ἔφυ & λείπεται); λείπομαι (> λείπω) – be inferior.

20 φίλ' (= φίλε *see l.8*); ἄνδρ' (= ἄνδρα) – *acc. in apposition to* σέ, *i.e. Hector*; ἀρκοῦντά (*from* ἀρκέω + *dat.*) – who was sufficient.

21 ξυνέσει – *see l.19*; γένος -ους τό (< genealogy) – lineage; πλοῦτος -ου ὁ (< plutocrat) – wealth; τε κἀνδρείᾳ (= τε καὶ ἀνδρείᾳ) (> ἀνδρεῖος) – *this noun and all the other datives in this line follow* μέγαν: *translate as* 'great in understanding, in lineage, and in both wealth and bravery'.

22 ἀκήρατος -ον – untouched, a virgin (*an example of a compound, 'two-termination', adjective, with only masc. & neut. endings*); δόμος – house (*see l.7*).

23 παρθένειος -ον (< Parthenon) – of a virgin; λέχος -ους τό – bed (*see l.13*); ἐζεύξω (*2nd sing. aorist mid. of* ζεύγνυμι) (> ζυγόν) – be united (have sex) with in marriage: *translate the whole clause as* 'you first were united with me in marriage on my virgin bed'.

24 ὄλωλας (*from* ὄλλυμι) – you are dead; ναυσθλοῦμαι – be carried by sea.
25 δοῦλον – (*here used as an adjective*) of a slave; ζυγόν – *see l.17*.
26 οὔπω – not yet (> οὐ); ναός = νεώς; σκάφος -ους τό – hull (of a boat).
27 γραφή -ῆς ἡ (< photograph) – picture; κλύουσ' (= κλύουσα) *from* κλύω (= ἀκούω) – hearing about it [*i.e. a boat*]; ἐπίσταμαι (< epistemology) – I understand.
28 ἤν = ἐάν (+ *subjunctive, indicating a general condition*) – if ever; μέτριος -α -ον – moderate (*followed by prolative infinitive* φέρειν 'to endure').
29 προθυμία -ας ἡ + *gen.* – eagerness for; σωθῆναι (*the infinitive explains the sailors' eagerness*) – so as to be saved; πόνος -ου ὁ – task, job.

Hecuba recommends that Andromache let circumstances take their course, relinquishing her devotion to Hector and focusing on her son (Trojan Women 690–708).

ὁ μὲν παρ' οἴαχ', ὁ δ' ἐπὶ λαίφεσιν βεβώς,	30
ὁ δ' ἄντλον εἴργων ναός· ἢν δ' ὑπερβάλῃ	
πολὺς ταραχθεὶς πόντος, ἐνδόντες τύχῃ	
παρεῖσαν αὑτοὺς κυμάτων δρομήμασιν.	
οὕτω δὲ κἀγὼ πόλλ' ἔχουσα πήματα	
ἄφθογγός εἰμι καὶ παρεῖσ' ἔχω στόμα·	35
νικᾷ γὰρ οὑκ θεῶν με δύστηνος κλύδων.	
ἀλλ', ὦ φίλη παῖ, τὰς μὲν Ἕκτορος τύχας	
ἔασον· οὐ μὴ δάκρυά νιν σώσῃ τὰ σά·	
τίμα δὲ τὸν παρόντα δεσπότην σέθεν,	
φίλον διδοῦσα δέλεαρ ἀνδρὶ σῶν τρόπων.	40
κἂν δρᾷς τάδ', ἐς τὸ κοινὸν εὐφρανεῖς φίλους	
καὶ παῖδα τόνδε παιδὸς ἐκθρέψειας ἂν	
Τροίᾳ μέγιστον ὠφέλημ', ἵν' οἵ ποτε	
ἐκ σοῦ γενόμενοι παῖδες Ἴλιον πάλιν	
κατοικίσειαν καὶ πόλις γένοιτ' ἔτι.	45
ἀλλ' ἐκ λόγου γὰρ ἄλλος ἐκβαίνει λόγος,	
τίν' αὖ δέδορκα τόνδ' Ἀχαιϊκὸν λάτριν	
στείχοντα καινῶν ἄγγελον βουλευμάτων;	

Place

Τροία -ας ἡ, Ἴλιον -ου τό: Troy. *Its alternative name, Ilium, lies behind the title given to Homer's great epic poem* The Iliad.

Gender and moral agency in Ancient Greece
Euripides was well-known for introducing moral and ethical ideas into his plays which reflected current topics of popular thinking. However, Hecuba's pragmatic argument (that a course of action with the most personal benefit is preferable to one with no achievable consequence) challenges contemporary Athenian debate on the right way to live: males may see their choice being shaped either, as in the world of Homer, by the individual's sense of the honour in which he is held by others and his rejection of anything which might damage it or, as in the world of the city-state (πόλις), by an obligation to the good of the community and behaviour that will be beneficial to more people. But for a female, particularly in a time of war, Euripides suggests there is little such choice, but merely the question of how best to endure what life brings.

> Q. What characteristics of sailors' behaviour does Hecuba use in her argument?
> Q. Do you agree with Hecuba's advice to her daughter? What factors may compel Andromache to follow her mother's recommendation?
> Q. What assumption lies behind Hecuba's comment on Andromache's son? Why do you think Euripides makes us aware of him at this point?

GCSE vocabulary: ἀγαθός (ἄριστος), ἀγγέλλω, ἄγγελος, ἀλλά, ἄλλος, ἄν, ἀνήρ, γάρ, γίγνομαι, δέ, δεσπότης, ἐάν, ἑαυτόν, ἐγώ, εἰμί, ἐκ, (ἐκ)βαίνω, ἔτι, θεός, ἵνα, καί, λόγος, μέγας, μέν... δέ..., νικάω, ὅδε, οὐ, οὕτω, παῖς, παρά, πόλις, πολύς, σός, σύ, σῴζω, τιμάω, τίς, τύχη, φίλος.

30   ὁ μέν... ὁ δ'... ὁ δ' – one man... another... another; **παρ' οἴαχ'** – to the tiller; **ἐπὶ λαίφεσιν** – to the sails; **βεβώς** (*perfect participle from* βαίνω) – having gone.
31   **ἄντλος -ου ὁ** – bilge water; **εἴργω** – pump out; **ἤν** = ἐάν + *subjunctive* (*the* δ' (δέ) *picks up the* μέν *in l.28*); **ὑπερβάλῃ** (*from* ὑπερβάλλω, *aorist* ὑπερέβαλον) – be excessive.
32   **ταραχθείς** *from* ταράττω – confuse; **πόντος -ου ὁ** – sea; **ἐνδόντες** (*aor. part. from* ἐνδίδωμι) + *dat.* – having given in (*referring to the sailors mentioned in l.30-1*).
33   **παρεῖσαν** (*from* παρίημι) – they surrender (*the aorist tense expresses a general truth*); **αὑτούς** = ἑαυτούς; **κῦμα -ατος τό** – wave; **δρόμημα -ατος τό** – surge, swell.
34   **κἀγώ** = καὶ ἐγώ (*see* crasis, *p.81*); **πῆμα -ατος τό** – misfortune.
35   **ἄφθογγός -ον** – speechless (*see l.18*); **παρεῖσ' ἔχω** (= παρεῖσα, *aorist participle of* παρίημι: *see* elision, *p.81*) – 'I have surrendered' (ἔχω + *aor. participle can be used to express a perfect tense*); **στόμα -ατος τό** (< stomata) – voice.
36   **οὐκ** (= ὁ ἐκ) *with* **κλύδων -ωνος ὁ** – a wave from...; **δύστηνος -ον** – disastrous.
38   **ἔασον** (*from* ἐάω, *aorist imperative*) – dismiss, let go; **οὐ μή** (+ *aorist subjunctive*, σώσῃ, *expresses a strong negative prediction*) – certainly will not; **δάκρυ -υος τό** (> δακρύω) – tear; **νιν** (= αὐτόν) – him.
39   **παρόντα** (*present participle of* πάρειμι) – who is present, current; **σέθεν** = σοῦ (*see* poetic forms, *p.81*).
40   **διδοῦσα** (*present participle of* δίδωμι) (> ἔδωκα) – offering; **φίλος** – pleasing (*see l.8*); **δέλεαρ -ατος τό** – enticement; **τρόπος -ου ὁ** (< trope) – character (*the plural here denotes the different elements of Andromache's character*).
41   **κἄν** = καὶ ἐάν (+ *subjunctive*); **δρᾷς** (*present subjunctive of* δράω) – you do; **ἐς τὸ κοινόν** – equally; **εὐφρανεῖς** (*future from* εὐφραίνω) – you will gladden.
42   **παῖδα τόνδε παιδός** – Hecuba's grandson is the son of Hector and Andromache and called Astyanax: the use of τόνδε shows he came on stage with Andromache; **ἐκθρέψειας ἄν** (*2nd sing. aorist optative from* ἐκτρέφω) – you would bring up (ἄν + *optative expresses a potential outcome*).
43   **ὠφέλημα -ατος τό** – as a benefit (*in apposition to* παῖδα *in l.42*); **οἵ ποτε** – take with παῖδες: 'those children who at some time'.
44   **πάλιν** (< palindrome) – again.
45   **κατοικίσειαν** (*3rd plur. aorist optative of* κατοικίζω; *in a purpose clause after* ἵνα *in l.43*) (> οἰκέω) – might found.
46   **ἀλλ'...ἄλλος** (*NB the different accentuation on these two words*) – but...further (another); **ἐκβαίνει** – *from* βαίνω.
47   **τίν'** = τίνα; **αὖ** – next (*here*); **δέδορκα** – I see; **λάτρις -ιος ὁ/ἡ** (*acc.* λάτριν) – servant.
48   **στείχω** – approach; **καινός -ή -όν** – new; **βούλευμα -ατος τό** – deliberation.

A herald from the Greek army, Talthybius, enters and the drama takes a different turn. His sense of shame prevents him from saying clearly what the Greeks have decreed, but he finally reveals what is to be the fate of Andromache and Hector's son (Trojan Women 709–25).

Talthybius	Φρυγῶν ἀρίστου πρίν ποθ' Ἕκτορος δάμαρ,	
	μή με στυγήσῃς· οὐχ ἑκὼν γὰρ ἀγγελῶ	50
	Δαναῶν τε κοινὰ Πελοπιδῶν τ' ἀγγέλματα.	
Andromache	τί δ' ἔστιν; ὥς μοι φροιμίων ἀρχὴ κακῶν.	
Talth.	ἔδοξε τόνδε παῖδα ... πῶς εἴπω λόγον;	
Andr.	μῶν οὐ τὸν αὐτὸν δεσπότην ἡμῖν ἔχειν;	
Talth.	οὐδεὶς Ἀχαιῶν τοῦδε δεσπόσει ποτέ.	55
Andr.	ἀλλ' ἐνθάδ' αὐτὸν λείψανον Φρυγῶν λιπεῖν;	
Talth.	οὐκ οἶδ' ὅπως σοι ῥᾳδίως εἴπω κακά.	
Andr.	ἐπῄνεσ' αἰδῶ, πλὴν ἐὰν λέγῃς κακά.	
Talth.	κτενοῦσι σὸν παῖδ', ὡς πύθῃ κακὸν μέγα.	
Andr.	οἴμοι, γάμων τόδ' ὡς κλύω μεῖζον κακόν.	60
Talth.	νικᾷ δ' Ὀδυσσεὺς ἐν Πανέλλησιν λέγων ...	
Andr.	αἰαῖ μάλ'· οὐ γὰρ μέτρια πάσχομεν κακά.	
Talth.	λέξας ἀρίστου παῖδα μὴ τρέφειν πατρός ...	
Andr.	τοιαῦτα νικήσειε τῶν αὑτοῦ πέρι.	
Talth.	ῥῖψαι δὲ πύργων δεῖν σφε Τρωϊκῶν ἄπο.	65

Names and places

Φρύγες -ων οἱ, Τρωϊκοί -ῶν οἱ: Trojans. *Troy is situated in what, in the Ancient World, was known as Phrygia.*

Δαναοί -ῶν οἱ, Ἀχαιοί -ῶν οἱ: Greeks. *Further alternative names in the Homeric style, anchoring Euripides' drama in its epic ancestor.*

Πελοπίδαι -ῶν οἱ: The descendants of Pelops. *This refers to Agamemnon and Menelaus, the Greek commanders-in-chief at Troy, grandsons of Pelops.*

Ὀδυσσεύς -έως ὁ: Odysseus, *the Greek hero famous for his cunning and skill with words.*

Πανέλληνες -ων οἱ: [Assembly of] all the Greeks

Stichomythia

This is the term (= 'one line of speech') used to describe a section of a Greek drama where the characters deliver one line in turn: it recreates the quickfire interaction of people conversing whilst in a heightened emotional state. When translating, note how the syntax of a statement made by one character in a line may be carried on either by the same character continuing his speech next time he speaks, or by the other character speaking in response; this may happen over several lines. Stichomythia must have given actors a chance to show off their skills.

GCSE vocabulary: ἀλλά, ἀπό, (ἀπο)κτείνω, ἄριστος (ἀγαθός), ἄρχομαι, αὐτός, γάρ, δέ, δεῖ, δεσπότης, δοκεῖ, ἐάν, ἑαυτόν, ἐγώ, εἰμί, ἐνθάδε, ἔχω, ἡμεῖς, κακός, λέγω, λείπω, λόγος, μέγας, μή, νικάω, ὅδε, οἶδα, οὐ, οὐδείς, παῖς, πάσχω, πατήρ, περί, πλήν, πυνθάνομαι, πῶς, ῥᾴδιος, σός, σύ, τίς, τοιοῦτος.

49 πρίν – formerly; ποθ' (= ποτε) – at one time; δάμαρ – wife (*see l.7*).
50 μή... στυγήσῃς (*from* στυγέω, *aorist subjunctive with* μή *denoting a prohibition*) – don't hate; ἑκών -οῦσα -όν – willing.
51 κοινός -ή -όν – shared; ἀγγέλμα -ατος τό (> ἄγγελος) – proclamation.
52 ὡς (*introducing an exclamation; it has gained its accent from* μοι) – how!; φροίμιον -ου τό (< proemium) – introduction (*plural for singular*).
53 ἔδοξε – supply αὐτοῖς (= *the Greeks etc. in l.51*); τόνδε παῖδα – *i.e. Astyanax*; εἴπω – am I to say (*the subjunctive shows that Talthybius is anxiously deliberating with himself*).
54 μῶν – surely not ... (*Andromache expresses her disbelief by using this word which expects the response to be negative*); οὐ... ἔχειν – that he is not to have (*the infinitive follows* ἔδοξε *in l.53, continuing Talthybius' words as he tries unsuccessfully to report the order given by the Greek commanders*).
55 δεσπόσει + gen. (> δεσπότης) – will be the master of; ποτέ – at any time (*see l.49*).
56 λείψανον -ου τό (> λείπω) – last remnant; λιπεῖν – *see l.54 on* ἔχειν (*Andromache again supplies a decree that Talthybius' commanders may have made*).
57 ὅπως – how (*introducing an indirect question*); εἴπω – *see l.53, more deliberation*.
58 ἐπήνεσ' (= ἐπῄνεσα *from* ἐπαινέω) – I approve (*compare l.14: the aorist is used here to indicate Andromache's current, momentary, frame of mind*); αἰδῶ (*acc. of* αἰδώς -οῦς ἡ) – consideration
59 ὡς + *subjunctive* – so that (ὡς – like ἵνα – *here introduces a purpose clause*).
60 οἴμοι – O no!; γάμος -ου ὁ (< bigamist) – marriage (*genitive of comparison after* μεῖζον, *plural for singular – Andromache refers to her future enslavement to Achilles' son as a marriage, compare l.7*); ὡς – how! (*see l.52*); κλύω = ἀκούω (*see l.24*).
61 Πανέλλησιν – dat. plur. (*see* poetic forms, *p.81*).
62 αἰαῖ μάλ' – O no! No! (μάλα *emphasises and redoubles the emotion of her cry*); μέτριος -α -ον – proportionate.
63 λέξας (*weak aorist participle of* λέγω, *agreeing with* Ὀδυσσεύς *in l.61*) – telling them (λέγω + *inf. in indirect command* = tell); τρέφω – bring up, rear.
64 τοιαῦτα νικήσειε (*aorist optative expressing a wish for the future*) – may he win such a victory; τῶν αὑτοῦ (τῶν *genitive after* πέρι: NB the rough breathing on αὑτοῦ = ἑαυτοῦ, *see l.33*) – his own (children).
65 ῥῖψαι (*aorist infinitive of* ῥίπτω, *after* δεῖν) – to hurl; πύργος -ου ὁ – tower; δεῖν (*infinitive in an indirect command after* λέξας *in l.63*); σφε = αὐτόν; ἄπο – placed after its noun: *compare* πέρι *in l.64*.

Q. How do Talthybius' opening words create a sense of foreboding?
Q. Do you have any sympathy for Talthybius? How well do you think he handles the situation?
Q. How does Euripides' use of stichomythia here contribute to the drama?

Having finally revealed what is to be her son's fate, Talthybius urges Andromache to accept the Greeks' decision calmly and to recognise what will be gained by doing so (Trojan Women 726–39).

ἀλλ' ὡς γενέσθω καὶ σοφωτέρα φανῇ·
μήτ' ἀντέχου τοῦδ', εὐγενῶς δ' ἄλγει κακοῖς,
μήτε σθένουσα μηδὲν ἰσχύειν δόκει.
ἔχεις γὰρ ἀλκὴν οὐδαμῇ· σκοπεῖν δὲ χρή·
πόλις τ' ὄλωλε καὶ πόσις, κρατῇ δὲ σύ,   70
ἡμεῖς δὲ πρὸς γυναῖκα μάρνασθαι μίαν
οἷοί τε. τούτων οὕνεκ' οὐ μάχης ἐρᾶν
οὐδ' αἰσχρὸν οὐδὲν οὐδ' ἐπίφθονόν σε δρᾶν
οὐδ' αὖ σ' Ἀχαιοῖς βούλομαι ῥίπτειν ἀράς.
εἰ γάρ τι λέξεις ὧν χολώσεται στρατός,   75
οὔτ' ἂν ταφείη παῖς ὅδ' οὔτ' οἴκτου τύχοι.
σιγῶσα δ' εὖ τε τὰς τύχας κεκτημένη
τὸν τοῦδε νεκρὸν οὐκ ἄθαπτον ἂν λίποις
αὐτή τ' Ἀχαιῶν πρευμενεστέρων τύχοις.

Odysseus in Greek tragedy

Odysseus is given quite contrasting characteristics in Greek tragedy, but they all have their origins in the persuasive cunning that characterises him in the Homeric poems. In some plays, his cunning persuades his fellows to make laudable choices which reinforce the qualities of a well-led state or army: in others, his cunning proves to be deceitful and self-serving, and illustrates the worst characteristics of the populist politicians in fifth-century Athens, known as 'demagogues', who provoked the scorn of opponents of her democratic system of government. Odysseus in *Trojan Women* seems to be closer to the latter type.

Loss of identity and descent into slavery

Talthybius' exhortation to Andromache not to pretend that she is stronger than she is not only derives from the fact that she is a single woman facing a multitude of armed men, but she also lacks both husband and city and has therefore lost the vital source of the identity and status of a free woman in Ancient Greek society. Andromache is thus reduced to the status of slave. She can only shape her behaviour and curb the expression of her grief to the whim of the men who are now dominant in her life. Andromache cannot act to save her child's life, but can merely act to determine how, perhaps, her child will be treated after his death. Euripides presents the pathos of the experience of a female survivor of a sacked city in a very powerful way.

- Q. How sympathetically does Talthybius speak to Andromache?
- Q. Consider how Talthybius uses different types of negative words to reinforce his points in these lines.
- Q. How, in the last five lines, does Euripides' wordplay emphasise that Andromache is in the hands of chance and has little agency in the way that events turn out?
- Q. In what ways does Andromache's situation echo that of a contemporary refugee?

> **GCSE vocabulary:** αἰσχρός, ἀλλά, ἄν, αὐτός, βούλομαι, γάρ, γενέσθω (γίγνομαι), γυνή, δέ, δοκεῖ (δοκεῖ), εἰ, εὖ, ἔχω, ἡμεῖς, θάπτω (ταφείη), καί, κακός, λέγω (λέξεις), λείπω, μάχη, μηδείς, μήτε… μήτε…, μίαν (εἷς), νεκρός, ὅδε, οἷοί τε (οἷός τ' εἰμί), ὅς, οὐ, οὐδείς, οὔτε… οὔτε…, οὗτος, παῖς, πόλις, πρός, σοφός (σοφωτέρα), στρατός, σύ, τε… καί…, τις, τύχη, φαίνομαι (φανῇ), χρή.

66 ὥς (= οὕτως) – like this; γενέσθω (*3rd sing. aor. imperative*) (> γίγνομαι) – let it happen.

67 μήτ' (= μήτε) + *present imperative* – *introduces the first of Talthybius' instructions*; ἀντέχου (*present imperative of* ἀντέχομαι) + *gen.* – resist; εὐγενῶς – nobly; ἄλγει (*imperative from* ἀλγέω: *NB the acute accent distinguishes this form from 3rd sing.* ἀλγεῖ) (< nostalgia) – grieve; κακοῖς – *dative expressing the cause of the grief*.

68 σθένουσα (*from* σθενέω) – *qualified by the adverbial* μηδέν *placed after it: translate as* 'when you are in no way strong'; ἰσχύω (> ἰσχυρός) – be strong; δόκει – think (*imperative of* δοκέω, *see* ἄλγει *in l.67*).

69 ἀλκή -ῆς ἡ – influence, strength; οὐδαμῇ – in no way (*see* poetic forms, *p.81*); σκοπέω (< microscope) – reflect; χρή – *understand* σε *here*.

70 ὄλωλε – is finished, destroyed (*see l.24*); πόσις (*compare l.1 & 9*) – husband; κρατέω – overpower.

71 πρός + *acc.* – against; μάρναμαι – fight, do battle.

72 οἷοί τε (*understand* ἐσμέν) – we are able; οὕνεκ' (= οὕνεκα; *preposition + gen., placed after its pronoun* τούτων) – in the light of [these things]; ἐράω (< erotic) + *gen.* – be in love with (*understand* σε *as the subject of the infinitive which is dependent on* βούλομαι *in l.74*).

73 οὐδ' = οὐδε (*see l.16*) – nor even; οὐδέν (*reinforcing the earlier negative*) – *translate as* 'anything'; ἐπίφθονος -ον – hateful; δράω (< drama) – do (*infinitive, dependent on* βούλομαι *in l.74*).

74 αὖ – moreover; ῥίπτω – hurl; ἀρά -ᾶς ἡ – curse.

75 εἰ – *conditional with future indicative implies a threat or warning*; τι… ὧν – anything of the things which; χολώσεται (*future passive of* χολόω) + *gen.* (< melancholy) – will be provoked to anger by.

76 ἂν ταφείη (*aorist optative passive of* θάπτω) (< cenotaph) – would be buried (ἄν + *optative denotes a potential outcome*); οἶκτος -ου ὁ – pity; τύχοι (*strong aorist optative active of* τυγχάνω, *again with* ἄν) + *gen.* (> τύχη) – meet with.

77 σιγῶσα (*present participle of* σιγάω, *replacing a conditional clause*) (> σιγή) – if you are calm; τε – and (*see l.3: here it links the two participles in l.77*); τύχας – misfortunes (*the plural, often indicating neutral fortune, here it is negative*); κεκτημένη (*perfect participle from* κτάομαι) – if you endure (*the participle replaces a conditional clause*).

78 ἄθαπτος -ον (> θάπτω) – unburied; ἄν (+ *optative*) – *see l.76*.

79 πρευμενής -ές – well-disposed; τύχοις – *see l.76: the potential* ἄν *is to be understood from l.78*.

Andromache addresses her child in a lament; her hopes at her wedding contrast starkly with the hopeless reality she and her child now face (Trojan Women 740–56).

Andromache	ὦ φίλτατ', ὦ περισσὰ τιμηθεὶς τέκνον,	80
	θανῇ πρὸς ἐχθρῶν μητέρ' ἀθλίαν λιπών,	
	ἡ τοῦ πατρὸς δέ σ' εὐγένει' ἀποκτενεῖ,	
	ἣ τοῖσιν ἄλλοις γίγνεται σωτηρία,	
	τὸ δ' ἐσθλὸν οὐκ ἐς καιρὸν ἦλθέ σοι πατρός.	
	ὦ λέκτρα τἀμὰ δυστυχῆ τε καὶ γάμοι,	85
	οἷς ἦλθον ἐς μέλαθρον Ἕκτορός ποτε,	
	οὐ σφάγιον υἱὸν Δαναΐδαις τέξουσ' ἐμόν,	
	ἀλλ' ὡς τύραννον Ἀσιάδος πολυσπόρου.	
	ὦ παῖ, δακρύεις; αἰσθάνῃ κακῶν σέθεν;	
	τί μου δέδραξαι χερσὶ κἀντέχῃ πέπλων,	90
	νεοσσὸς ὡσεὶ πτέρυγας ἐσπίτνων ἐμάς;	
	οὐκ εἶσιν Ἕκτωρ κλεινὸν ἁρπάσας δόρυ	
	γῆς ἐξανελθὼν σοὶ φέρων σωτηρίαν,	
	οὐ συγγένεια πατρός, οὐκ ἰσχὺς Φρυγῶν·	
	λυγρὸν δὲ πήδημ' ἐς τράχηλον ὑψόθεν	95
	πεσὼν ἀνοίκτως πνεῦμ' ἀπορρήξεις σέθεν.	

Names and places
Δαναΐδαι -ων οἱ: Greeks. *This title refers to the mythical figure, Danaus, whose descendants were the Greeks of Argos and the surrounding area, which included Mycenae, home of Agamemnon.*

Ἀσιάς -άδος ἡ: Asia. *This was the geographical area in which Troy was situated.*

The precariousness of good fortune
In Homer's *Iliad* book 22, on finding out about the death of Hector, Andromache immediately considers how her son will lose the privileges which were his birthright now that his father, source and protector of those privileges, has died. But in Euripides' play she must confront what his paternal privileges bring in a tragically different way. Hector's son will be brutally killed for no other reason than that he is Hector's son: he must be prevented from living to avenge the death of his father.

The spirits of the dead
Athenians of the fifth century BCE were acutely aware of the spirits of their dead, as Andromache is of Hector here. While burial guaranteed the peace of the departed soul and its transition from a physical to spiritual state, it was clearly recognised that a return was unlikely. Indeed, any such interaction depended on very particular, magical, and frightening, circumstances, as Odysseus' experience with the souls of the dead in *Odyssey* book 11 makes very clear.

> **GCSE vocabulary:** αἰσθάνομαι, ἀλλά, ἄλλος, ἀποκτείνω, γῆ, γίγνομαι, δακρύω, δέ, δυστυχής, ἔρχομαι (ἦλθε), ἐγώ, εἰμι, ἐμός, ἐχθρός, κακός, λείπω, μήτηρ, ὅς, οὐ, παῖς, πατήρ, πίπτω, σύ, τε... καί..., τιμάω, τίς, υἱός, φέρω, χείρ, ὡς.

80 φίλτατ' (= φίλτατε, *vocative sing. of* φίλτατος, *superlative of* φίλος, *see l.8*) – dearest one; περισσά – exceedingly, too much; τιμηθείς – *although* τέκνον *is neuter, the masculine aorist participle here is easily understood to agree with it*; τέκνον -ου τό – child.

81 θανῇ (*future from* ἀποθνῄσκω) – you will die; πρός + *gen.* – at the hands of; ἀθλίος -α -ον – wretched.

82 τοῦ πατρός – paternal; εὐγένεια -ας ἡ (< eugenics) – nobility.

83 τοῖσιν = τοῖς; σωτηρία -ας ἡ – salvation.

84 ἐσθλός -ή -όν – noble (*the use of the neuter article with the adjective generates the abstract noun*); ἐς καιρὸν ἦλθε σοί – 'turned out to your advantage'.

85 λέκτρον -ου τό (*compare l.15*) – (marriage-)bed; τἀμά = τὰ ἐμά (crasis); γάμος -ου ὁ (< monogamous) – wedding (*both nouns are plural for singular*).

86 οἷς – *dative expressing purpose*; ἐς = εἰς; μέλαθρον -ου τό – palace; ποτε (*without accent*) – at some time.

87 σφάγιον -ου τό – sacrificial victim; τέξουσ' (= τέξουσα, *future active participle of* τίκτω, *expressing purpose*) – with the intention of giving birth to.

88 τύραννος -ου ὁ (< tyrant) – king; πολύσπορος -ον – fruitful.

89 σέθεν = σοῦ (*see l.39*).

90 τί – why? (*here*); δέδραξαι (*perfect of* δράσσομαι) + *gen.* – have you grasped; ἀντέχομαι + *gen.* – cling to; πέπλος -ου ὁ – robe.

91 νεοσσός -οῦ ὁ – young bird, chick; ὡσεί – like; πτέρυξ -υγος ἡ – wing; ἐσπίτνων (= εἰσπίπτων) – huddling up under.

92 κλεινός -ή -όν – famous; ἁρπάζω (< harpy) – seize hold of; δόρυ -ατος τό – spear.

93 ἐξανελθών (*the two prefixes* ἐκ & ἀνά *are very expressive here*) + *gen.* – coming up out of; σωτηρίαν – *see l.83*.

94 συγγένεια -ας ἡ – kinsmen (*the abstract noun, meaning* 'kinship', *expresses the factor that kinsmen share*); ἰσχύς -ύος ἡ – power.

95 λυγρός -ά -όν – tragic; πήδημα -ατος τό – fall (*lit.* 'a leap'); ἐς = εἰς; τράχηλος -ου ὁ – neck; ὑψόθεν – from a height: *translate the line with* πεσών *in l.96* 'having broken your neck in a tragic fall from a height'.

96 ἀνοίκτως – with nobody to pity you; πνεῦμα -ατος τό (< pneumatic) – (life's) breath; ἀπορρήξεις (*future indicative active of* ἀπορρήγνυμι) – you will choke off; σέθεν = σοῦ (*see l.39*).

> Q. Why does Hector remain so much the focus of Andromache as she expresses her grief in these lines?
>
> Q. Which features of Andromache's lament show how young her son is?
>
> Q. What do you make of Andromache's words in lines 89–96? How would you direct an actor to deliver them?

Andromache continues to say goodbye to her son and curses the Greeks, in particular Helen, for this act of barbaric cruelty (Trojan Women 757–69).

ὦ νέον ὑπαγκάλισμα μητρὶ φίλτατον,
ὦ χρωτὸς ἡδὺ πνεῦμα· διὰ κενῆς ἄρα
ἐν σπαργάνοις σε μαστὸς ἐξέθρεψ' ὅδε,
μάτην δ' ἐμόχθουν καὶ κατεξάνθην πόνοις.   100
νῦν, οὔποτ' αὖθις, μητέρ' ἀσπάζου σέθεν,
πρόσπιτνε τὴν τεκοῦσαν, ἀμφὶ δ' ὠλένας
ἕλισσ' ἐμοῖς νώτοισι καὶ στόμ' ἅρμοσον.
ὦ βάρβαρ' ἐξευρόντες Ἕλληνες κακά,
τί τόνδε παῖδα κτείνετ' οὐδὲν αἴτιον;   105
ὦ Τυνδάρειον ἔρνος, οὔποτ' εἶ Διός,
πολλῶν δὲ πατέρων φημί σ' ἐκπεφυκέναι,
Ἀλάστορος μὲν πρῶτον, εἶτα δὲ Φθόνου,
Φόνου τε Θανάτου θ' ὅσα τε γῆ τρέφει κακά.

Names and places
Ἕλληνες -ων οἱ: Greeks. *This title reflects their descent from Hellen, the son of Pyrrha and Deucalion, the only survivors of the flood with which Zeus destroyed the human race.*

Τυνδάρειος -α -ον: of Tyndareus. *Tyndareus was married to Leda, and so was the mortal father of Helen, the wife of Menelaus whose abduction by Paris, son of Priam, caused the Trojan war.*

Ζεύς Διός (acc. Ζῆνα) ὁ: Zeus. *The father of the gods: he raped Leda soon after she had been impregnated by her husband, Tyndareus, and so was the immortal father of Leda's children.*

Helen
Famously 'the face that launched a thousand ships', Helen claimed to be the innocent victim of Paris' abduction but was hated by Andromache and the other Trojan women as the individual responsible for the disaster experienced by their people. Andromache here shows her hatred by denying the possibility that Helen could be one of the divine offspring of her mother Leda by Zeus (see above): if her parentage is divine, it is not of Zeus, but of immortal, abstract, personifications of evil.

Greek and barbarian
Originally, the Greek word βάρβαρος, reflecting the incomprehensible 'bar-bar' sounds of a non-Greek speaker, was the word for the 'non-Greek'. It had no value judgement attached (e.g. 'uncultured', 'cruel'). But, after the Greeks drove back the Persian invasions, a sense that what was non-Greek was also inferior took root. This notion was increased with the rising awareness, in the Athenian mind, that tyranny was the polar opposite to Athens' democracy and was also a feature of what was non-Greek (e.g. the Persian King). Where the decisions of a democracy are consensual and rational, those of an autocrat are random and self-serving. 'Barbaric' and 'Greek' became emotionally charged antonyms.

> **GCSE vocabulary:** αἴτιος, αὖθις, βάρβαροι, γάρ, γῆ, δέ, διά, εἰμί, Ἕλλην, ἐμός, Ζεύς, ἡδύς, θάνατος, κακός, μέν... δέ..., μήτηρ, νέος, νῦν, ὅδε, οὐ, οὐδείς, παῖς, πατήρ, πολύς, πρῶτος, σύ, τίς, φημί.

97 ὦ – Andromache exclaims her grief, also at l.98, 104, 106; ὑπαγκάλισμα -ατος τό – beloved (*literally: something which is hugged in the crook of the arms*); φίλτατος – dearest (*see l.80*).

98 χρώς -ωτός ὁ – skin; πνεῦμα -ατος τό (< pneumatic) – scent; διὰ κενῆς (*adverbial*) – in vain; ἆρα (*emphasising enclitic particle – NB different accentuation to interrogative* ἆρα) – for sure, indeed.

99 σπάργανα -ων τά – swaddling clothes (*material babies would be wrapped in*); μαστός -οῦ ὁ (< mastitis) – breast; ἐξέθρεψ' (= ἐξέθρεψε, *3rd sing. aorist indic. active of* ἐκτρέφω: *compare l.42*) – nursed.

100 μάτην – in vain; μοχθέω – labour; κατεξάνθην (*1st sing. aorist indicative passive of* καταξαίνω) – was I torn apart, racked (*literally, the verb expresses the process of pulling raw wool apart with a 'carding comb'*); πόνος -ου ὁ – labour.

101 οὔποτ' = οὐδέποτε; ἀσπάζομαι – kiss, hug; σέθεν = σου.

102 προσπίτνω (= προσπίπτω; *compare l.91*) – embrace; τεκοῦσα -ης ἡ – mother (*literally 'she who gave birth to you'*); ἀμφί (*take closely with the verb* ἕλισσε *in l.103: such separation of prepositional prefix from verb is called tmesis*) + *dat.* – around; ὠλένη -ης ἡ – arm.

103 ἑλίσσω (< helix) – entwine, wrap; νῶτος -ου ὁ – back (*plural for singular*); στόμ' ἅρμοσον (στόμα < stomatology) – join your mouth to mine!

104 ἐξευρόντες (*compound from* εὑρίσκω) – who have devised.

105 τί – why? (*see l.90*); κτείνετ' = ἀποκτείνετε; οὐδέν (*the neuter singular form is adverbial, qualifying* αἴτιον) – not at all.

106 ἔρνος -ους τό – offspring; οὔποτ' – *see l.101*.

107 ἐκπεφυκέναι (*infinitive in indirect speech after* φημί) + *gen.* – are born from.

108 Ἀλάστωρ -ορος ὁ – a Spirit of Destruction; εἶτα = ἔπειτα; Φθόνος -ου ὁ – Malice (*Andromache personifies the abstract spirit of ill-will*).

109 Φόνος -ου ὁ – Slaughter (*the personification of l.108 continues*); θ' (= τε) – and (*see l.1*); ὅσοι -αι -α – as many ... as (κακά *agrees with it*); τρέφω – nurture (*compare l.99*).

> Q. What aspect of Andromache's words in lines 97–103 do you find most moving?
> Q. How does Andromache use Helen's paternity to demonstrate the hatred she feels for her?
> Q Is it fair for Andromache to blame Helen for what happens to her son?

Andromache completes her abuse of Helen; she hands her son over to his death and demands to be taken on board ship to 'marriage' with a Greek (Trojan Women 770–9).

οὐ γάρ ποτ' αὐχῶ Ζῆνά γ' ἐκφῦσαί σ' ἐγώ,   110
πολλοῖσι κῆρα βαρβάροις Ἕλλησί τε.
ὄλοιο· καλλίστων γὰρ ὀμμάτων ἄπο
αἰσχρῶς τὰ κλεινὰ πεδί' ἀπώλεσας Φρυγῶν.
ἀλλ' ἄγετε φέρετε ῥίπτετ', εἰ ῥίπτειν δοκεῖ·
δαίνυσθε τοῦδε σάρκας. ἔκ τε γὰρ θεῶν   115
διολλύμεσθα, παιδί τ' οὐ δυναίμεθ' ἂν
θάνατον ἀρῆξαι. κρύπτετ' ἄθλιον δέμας
καὶ ῥίπτετ' ἐς ναῦς· ἐπὶ καλὸν γὰρ ἔρχομαι
ὑμέναιον, ἀπολέσασα τοὐμαυτῆς τέκνον.

Ancient Greek marriage

A marriage in fifth-century Athens was a private arrangement whereby a woman was passed from the oversight of one male (father, brother, or the closest male relative) to that of another (the bridegroom). Marriage was living together and so was considered to begin the moment that the bride was first brought to her husband's home. Aged from as young as 14 years old, she would be accompanied on this journey by a procession of other girls singing a song proclaiming her maidenly virtues; this song was sung and named in honour of the god of marriage, Hymenaeus.

> Q. What different emotions does Andromache reveal in these lines? How might you direct an actor to convey them effectively?
>
> Q. Why does the verb ῥίπτω feature so prominently in her words here?

Figure 11 *Andromache brings Hecuba news of the death of the Trojan princess Polyxena just before the extract from Euripides' play* The Trojan Women *begins: her slaughter/ sacrifice at the tomb of Achilles is depicted in all its wanton violence here on the Polyxena Sarcophagus, marble, c. 500–490* BCE, *excavated near to the site of Troy.*
Photo: Wikimedia (Dosseman).

> **GCSE vocabulary:** ἄγω, αἰσχρός (αἰσχρῶς), ἄν, ἀπό, γάρ, δοκεῖ, ἐγώ, εἰ, ἔκ, ἐπί, ἔρχομαι, θάνατος, θεός, καί, καλός (κάλλιστος), κρύπτω, ναῦς, ὅδε, οὐ, παῖς, πολύς, σύ, φέρω.

110 οὐ... ποτ' (= οὔποτε) – never (*see l.101 & 106: as with* φημί, *the negative is translated within the reported speech, not with the verb of speaking*); αὐχέω – assert with confidence; ἐκφύω (< physical) – father (*verb: compare l.107*).

111 κήρ -ος ἡ – an agent of death (*in apposition to* σε, *i.e. Helen, in l.110*); τε – and (*see l.3; here it links the two nouns* βαρβάροις *and* Ἕλλησί).

112 ὄλοιο (*aorist optative of* ὄλλυμαι, *expressing a wish for the future*) – I wish you dead; ὄμμα -ατος τό – eye (*viewed as the source of Helen's great beauty*).

113 κλεινός -ή -όν – famous; πεδίον -ου τό – plain; ἀπώλεσας (*aorist indicative active of* ἀπόλλυμι, *compare l.5 and l.112*) – you destroyed; ἄπο + gen. – (*here*) because of (*NB the preposition is placed after its noun, see l.64*).

114 ῥίπτω – hurl (*see l.65; the plural imperative shows that Andromache addresses the Greeks in general, even though Talthybius, their representative, is onstage alone; the object of the three imperatives is understood to be 'him', referring to Astyanax*).

115 δαίνυμαι (δαίνυσθε, *2nd plur. pres. imperative*) – feast on; σάρξ σαρκός ἡ (< sarcophagus) – flesh; τε – *take with the* τ' *in l.116 to link the verb clauses*; ἔκ + gen. – because of (*here conveys the origin of her suffering*).

116 διολλύμεσθα (*compare l.112 and l.113: 1st plural present passive of* διολλύμι, *see* poetic forms *p.81: plural for singular, she is only speaking of herself*) – I am utterly ruined; δυναίμεθ' (= δυναίμεθα, *1st plural present optative of* δύναμαι: *plural for singular again*) – I would not be able to (*as in e.g. l.42 and ll.78–9,* ἄν + *optative denotes a potential outcome. Here it suggests that, even if she had the capacity to bring about the outcome, the involvement of the gods would prevent her*).

117 ἀρήγω – keep X (*acc.*) from Y (*dat.*); κρύπτετ' (< cryptic) = κρύπτετε (*Andromache now turns to address the chorus: she wants them to cover her with a veil, as if for her marriage*); ἄθλιος -α -ον – wretched (*see l.81*); δέμας τό – body.

118 ῥίπτω – *compare l.114*; ἐς = εἰς; ἐπί + acc. – to.

119 ὑμέναιος -ου ὁ – wedding song (*and therefore* 'wedding'); ἀπολέσασα (*see l.113, aorist active participle*) – having lost; τοὐμαυτῆς (= τό ἐμαυτῆς: crasis) – my own; τέκνον -ου τό – child (*see l.80*).

What happens next?

As soon as Andromache finishes her speech, she is escorted offstage in one direction to board Neoptolemus' ship, while her son, Astyanax, is taken away by Talthybius in the other to his death. Hecuba remains on stage, just as she will be throughout the play.

After the chorus has lamented Troy's chequered history and the destruction the city now faces, Menelaus enters and speaks of his wish to punish his disloyal wife,

Helen, with death. Hecuba does not trust Menelaus to resist the beauty and cunning of his wife and gets his consent to respond to Helen's plea for mercy. The two women present their arguments; despite the force of Hecuba's rejection of Helen's claim that she was the hapless victim of the power of the goddess Aphrodite, we suspect that, after Menelaus decides to postpone his revenge until after he arrives back in Greece, Helen will win him round and be spared.

Talthybius returns to the stage with the corpse of little Astyanax on his father Hector's shield. Hecuba is told to prepare her grandson for burial as best she can: the barbarism of the Greeks killing a helpless child for fear of what he might possibly do sometime in the future, and the tragedy of his short life, are the themes of her funerary lament. The chorus joins Hecuba in conducting the ritual of preparing the child's body.

Talthybius relays the orders for the Greek troops in Troy to set the final fires alight in the city and its citadel. As the fires burn down their home behind them, Hecuba and the chorus sing of their sorrow at the destruction of a once-great city. As the city collapses, the women – a queen, mothers, wives, and daughters – are led off stage to the Greek ships and into slavery. Even as Hecuba questions the existence of gods who seem to have ignored her sacrifices and prayers over the years we, the audience, are aware of the pact between Athena and Poseidon at the start of the play which will destroy so many of the Greeks in their hour of victory.

Final questions

- Why does Euripides give the pivotal central role in *Trojan Women* to Hecuba?
- Through which individual characters within the play may the voice be heard of the different roles taken by women in Athenian society – mother, wife, daughter, bride, mourner?
- If Euripides' play has a message for the victors of war at their moment of triumph and therefore of greatest confidence, what might it be?
- It has been said that Greek tragedy gives words to what might otherwise be an extended scream of agony: in what ways might this be particularly true of *Trojan Women*?
- With what events of recent world history does *Trojan Women* particularly resonate?
- What aspects of Euripides' play might present particular difficulties to a production today?

OCR GREEK GCSE DEFINED VOCABULARY LIST

A
ἀγαθός, ἀγαθή, ἀγαθόν	good
ἀγγέλλω, ἀγγελῶ, ἤγγειλα, ἠγγέλθην	I announce
ἄγγελος, ἀγγέλου, ὁ	messenger
ἀγορά, ἀγορᾶς, ἡ	market-place
ἀγρός, ἀγροῦ, ὁ	field, countryside
ἄγω, ἄξω, ἤγαγον, ἤχθην	I lead, bring
ἀγών, ἀγῶνος, ὁ	contest, trial
ἀδικέω	I do wrong, injure
ἄδικος, ἄδικος, ἄδικον	unjust, wrong
ἀεί	always
Ἀθῆναι, Ἀθηνῶν, αἱ	Athens
Ἀθηναῖοι, Ἀθηναίων, οἱ	the Athenians
Ἀθηναῖος, Ἀθηναία, Ἀθηναῖον	Athenian
ἆθλον, ἄθλου, τό	prize, reward
αἱρέω, αἱρήσω, εἷλον, ᾑρέθην	I take
αἰσθάνομαι, αἰσθήσομαι, ᾐσθόμην	I notice, perceive
αἰσχρός, αἰσχρά, αἰσχρόν	shameful, ugly, disgraceful
αἰτέω	I ask, ask for
αἴτιος, αἰτία, αἴτιον + gen.	responsible for, guilty of
αἰχμάλωτος, αἰχμαλώτου, ὁ	prisoner (of war)
ἀκούω, ἀκούσομαι, ἤκουσα, ἠκούσθην	I hear, listen
ἀληθής, ἀληθής, ἀληθές	true
ἀλλά	but
ἄλλος, ἄλλη, ἄλλο	other, another
ἄν	[*in conditional sentence, makes aorist verb mean* 'would have . . .']
ἀνά + acc.	up
ἀναγκάζω, ἀναγκάσω, ἠνάγκασα, ἠναγκάσθην	I force, compel
ἀναχωρέω	I retreat, withdraw
ἀνδρεῖος, ἀνδρεία, ἀνδρεῖον	brave, manly

ἄνεμος, ἀνέμου, ὁ	wind
ἄνευ + gen.	without
ἀνήρ, ἀνδρός, ὁ	man, husband
ἄνθρωπος, ἀνθρώπου, ὁ	man, person
ἄξιος, ἀξία, ἄξιον + gen.	worthy of, deserving
ἀπό + gen.	from, away from
ἀποθνῄσκω, ἀποθανοῦμαι, ἀπέθανον	I die, am killed
ἀποκρίνομαι, ἀποκρινοῦμαι, ἀπεκρινάμην	I reply, answer
ἀποκτείνω, ἀποκτενῶ, ἀπέκτεινα	I kill
ἆρα;	[introduces a question]
ἀρχή, ἀρχῆς, ἡ	beginning, rule, power, empire
ἄρχω + gen.	I rule
ἄρχομαι + gen.	I begin
ἄρχων, ἄρχοντος, ὁ	ruler, magistrate
ἀσθενής, ἀσθενής, ἀσθενές	weak
ἀσπίς, ἀσπίδος, ἡ	shield
ἀσφαλής, ἀσφαλής, ἀσφαλές	safe
αὖθις	again, in turn
αὐτός, αὐτή, αὐτό	self, himself, herself, itself (*emphatic*)
ὁ αὐτός, ἡ αὐτή, τὸ αὐτό	the same
αὐτόν, αὐτήν, αὐτό (acc./gen./dat. only – also plural)	him, her, it, them
ἀφικνέομαι, ἀφίξομαι, ἀφικόμην	I arrive

Β

βαίνω, βήσομαι, ἔβην	I go
βάλλω, βαλῶ, ἔβαλον, ἐβλήθην	I throw, fire at, hit (with missile)
βάρβαροι, βαρβάρων, οἱ	foreigners, barbarians, non-Greek
βασιλεύς, βασιλέως, ὁ	king
βία, βίας, ἡ	force, strength
βίβλος, βίβλου, ἡ	book
βίος, βίου, ὁ	life
βλάπτω	I harm, damage
βοάω	I shout
βοή, βοῆς, ἡ	shout
βοηθέω + dat.	I help, come to help
βουλή, βουλῆς, ἡ	plan, a council
βούλομαι, βουλήσομαι, ἐβουλήθην	I wish
βραδύς, βραδεῖα, βραδύ	slow

Γ

γάρ	for
γε	at any rate, even, at least
γελάω, γελάσομαι, ἐγέλασα	I laugh
γέρων, γέροντος, ὁ	old man
γῆ, γῆς, ἡ	land, earth
γίγνομαι, γενήσομαι, ἐγενόμην	I become, happen, occur
γιγνώσκω, γνώσομαι, ἔγνων, ἐγνώσθην	I know, realise, understand
γλῶσσα, γλώσσης, ἡ	tongue, language
γράφω	I write, draw
γυνή, γυναικός, ἡ	woman, wife

Δ

δακρύω	I cry, weep
δέ	but, and
δεῖ, δεήσει, ἐδέησε (with acc.+ infin.)	it is necessary
δεινός, δεινή, δεινόν	terrible, strange, clever
δεῖπνον, δείπνου, τό	dinner, meal
δέκα	ten
δένδρον, δένδρου, τό	tree
δεσπότης, δεσπότου, ὁ	master
δεύτερος, δευτέρα, δεύτερον	second
δέχομαι, δέξομαι, ἐδεξάμην	I receive, welcome
δή	indeed
δῆμος, δήμου, ὁ	people, community
διά + acc.	because of, on account of
διὰ τί;	why?
διά + gen.	through
δι' ὀλίγου	soon
διαφθείρω, διαφθερῶ, διέφθειρα, διεφθάρην	I destroy, corrupt
(δίδωμι), δώσω, ἔδωκα	I give (*future and aorist indicative active and infinitives only*)
δίκαιος, δικαία, δίκαιον	just, fair, upright
διδάσκω, διδάξω, ἐδίδαξα, ἐδιδάχθην	I teach, tell
διότι	because
διώκω	I chase, pursue, prosecute
δοκεῖ (μοι), δόξει, ἔδοξε	(I) decide (= it seems good (to me))
δοῦλος, δούλου, ὁ	slave
δοῦναι (cf. δίδωμι)	to give, to have given (*aor infin*)

δύο, δύο, δύο	two
δυστυχής, δυστυχής, δυστυχές	unlucky
δῶρον, δώρου, τό	present, gift

E

ἐάν	if
ἑαυτόν, ἑαυτήν, ἑαυτό	himself, herself, itself, *plural* themselves (*reflexive*)
ἐγώ, ἐμοῦ	I, (*acc.etc*) me
ἐμός, ἐμή, ἐμόν	my
ἐθέλω, ἐθελήσω, ἠθέλησα	I wish, am willing
εἰ	if
εἰδέναι (cf. οἶδα)	to know
εἰδώς, εἰδυῖα, εἰδός (cf. οἶδα)	knowing
εἰμί, ἔσομαι, ἦν (imperfect)	I am
εἶμι (cf. ἔρχομαι)	I shall go
εἰρήνη, εἰρήνης, ἡ	peace
εἰς + acc.	to, into
εἰς τοσοῦτον	to such an extent
εἷς, μία, ἕν	one
εἰσβάλλω	I throw into, invade
ἐκ or ἐξ + gen.	out of, from
ἕκαστος, ἑκάστη, ἕκαστον	each
ἐκεῖ	there
ἐκεῖνος, ἐκείνη, ἐκεῖνο	that, *plural* those
ἐκκλησία, ἐκκλησίας, ἡ	assembly, meeting
ἐκφεύγω	I escape
ἐλεύθερος, ἐλευθέρα, ἐλεύθερον	free
Ἑλλάς, Ἑλλάδος, ἡ	Greece
Ἕλλην, Ἕλληνος, ὁ	a Greek, Greek man
ἐλπίζω, ἐλπιῶ, ἤλπισα	I hope, expect
ἐν + dat.	in, among
ἐνθάδε	here, there
ἐννέα	nine
ἔνοικος, ἐνοίκου, ὁ	inhabitant
ἕξ	six
ἔξεστι(ν) (μοι)	I am allowed, I can (= it is permitted to me/ possible for me)
ἐπεί	when, since
ἔπειτα	then, afterwards
ἐπί + acc.	against, onto, on, at

ἐπιστολή, ἐπιστολῆς, ἡ	letter
ἕπομαι, ἕψομαι, ἑσπόμην + dat.	I follow
ἑπτά	seven
ἔργον, ἔργου, τό	work, task, deed, action
ἔρχομαι, εἶμι, ἦλθον	I go, come
ἐρωτάω, ἐρωτήσω, ἠρόμην (or ἠρώτησα)	I ask (a question)
ἐσθίω, (ἔδομαι), ἔφαγον	I eat
ἑσπέρα, ἑσπέρας, ἡ	evening
ἔτι	still, yet
ἕτοιμος, ἑτοίμη, ἕτοιμον	ready
ἔτος, ἔτους, τό	year
εὖ	well
εὐθύς	immediately, at once
εὑρίσκω, εὑρήσω, ηὗρον, ηὑρέθην	I find
εὐρύς, εὐρεῖα, εὐρύ	wide, broad
εὐτυχής, εὐτυχής, εὐτυχές	lucky, fortunate
ἔφη (cf. φήμι)	he/she said (*with direct speech*)
ἐχθρός, ἐχθρά, ἐχθρόν	hostile
ἐχθρός, ἐχθροῦ, ὁ	(personal) enemy
ἔχω (imperfect εἶχον), ἕξω, ἔσχον	I have
ἕως	while, until

Z

Ζεύς, Διός, ὁ	Zeus
ζητέω	I seek

H

ἤ	or, than
ἤ . . . ἤ	either . . . or . . .
ἡγεμών, ἡγεμόνος, ὁ	guide, leader
ἤδη	already, by now
ἡδύς, ἡδεῖα, ἡδύ	pleasant, sweet
ἡμεῖς, ἡμῶν	we, (*acc.etc*) us
ἡμέτερος, ἡμετέρα, ἡμέτερον	our
ἡμέρα, ἡμέρας, ἡ	day

Θ

θάλασσα, θαλάσσης, ἡ	sea
θάνατος, θανάτου, ὁ	death
θάπτω, θάψω, ἔθαψα	I bury

θαυμάζω	I am amazed at, admire
θεά, θεᾶς, ἡ	goddess
θεός, θεοῦ, ὁ	god
θυγάτηρ, θυγατρός, ἡ	daughter
θύρα, θύρας, ἡ	door
θύω	I sacrifice

Ι

ἰατρός, ἰατροῦ, ὁ	doctor
ἰέναι (cf. εἶμι)	to go
ἱερόν, ἱεροῦ, τό	temple
ἱερός, ἱερά, ἱερόν	sacred, holy
ἵνα + subj. or opt.	in order that, in order to
ἱππεύς, ἱππέως, ὁ	cavalryman, *in plural* (the) cavalry
ἵππος, ἵππου, ὁ	horse
ἰσχυρός, ἰσχυρά, ἰσχυρόν	strong
ἰών, ἰοῦσα, ἰόν (cf. εἶμι)	going

Κ

καθεύδω	I sleep
καθίζω, καθιῶ, ἐκάθισα	I (make to) sit down
καί	and, also, even, too
καίπερ + participle	although
καίω, καύσω, ἔκαυσα, ἐκαύθην	I burn, set on fire
κακός, κακή, κακόν	bad, wicked, cowardly
καλέω, καλῶ, ἐκάλεσα, ἐκλήθην	I call, summon
καλός, καλή, καλόν	beautiful, handsome, fine
κατά + acc.	according to, by, down, along
κατὰ γῆν	by land
κατὰ θάλασσαν	by sea
κατά + gen.	down, down from
κελεύω	I order
κεφαλή, κεφαλῆς, ἡ	head
κίνδυνος, κινδύνου, ὁ	danger
κλέπτω, κλέψω, ἔκλεψα, ἐκλάπην	I steal
κολάζω	I punish
κόπτω, κόψω, ἔκοψα	I cut (down)
κρύπτω	I hide (something)
κρύπτομαι	I hide (myself)

κτάομαι, κτήσομαι, ἐκτησάμην	I obtain, get
κωλύω + infin.	I hinder, prevent (someone from doing)

Λ

λάθρᾳ	in secret, secretly
Λακεδαιμόνιοι, Λακεδαιμονίων, οἱ	the Spartans
λαμβάνω, λήψομαι, ἔλαβον, ἐλήφθην	I take, capture
λέγω, ἐρῶ, εἶπον, ἐρρήθην	I say, speak, tell
λείπω, λείψω, ἔλιπον, ἐλείφθην	I leave (behind)
λίθος, λίθου, ὁ	stone
λιμήν, λιμένος, ὁ	harbour
λόγος, λόγου, ὁ	word, speech, argument, story, account, reason
λύω	I loose, untie, set free

M

μάλιστα	most, very much, especially
μᾶλλον	more
μανθάνω, μαθήσομαι, ἔμαθον	I learn, understand
μάχη, μάχης, ἡ	battle, fight
μάχομαι, μαχοῦμαι, ἐμαχεσάμην	I fight
μέγας, μεγάλη, μέγα	big, great
μέλλω, μελλήσω, ἐμέλλησα + fut. infin.	I intend, am going to, hesitate
... μέν ... δέ	[*marks a contrast*]
μέντοι	however
μένω, μενῶ, ἔμεινα	I wait, remain
μετά + acc.	after
μετά + gen.	with
μή	not
μηδείς, μηδεμία, μηδέν	no-one, nothing, no
μηδέποτε	never
μήτε ... μήτε ...	neither ... nor ...
μήτηρ, μητρός, ἡ	mother
μικρός, μικρά, μικρόν	little, small
μισέω	I hate
μόνος, μόνη, μόνον	alone, only
μόνον	only
μῦθος, μύθου, ὁ	story
μῶρος, μώρα, μῶρον	foolish, stupid

Ν

ναῦς, νεώς, ἡ	ship, warship
ναύτης, ναύτου, ὁ	sailor
ναυτικόν, ναυτικοῦ, τό	fleet
νεανίας, νεανίου, ὁ	young man
νεκρός, νεκροῦ, ὁ	corpse
νέος, νέα, νέον	new, young, recent
νῆσος, νήσου, ἡ	island
νικάω	I win, conquer
νίκη, νίκης, ἡ	victory
νομίζω, νομιῶ, ἐνόμισα	I think, consider, believe
νόμος, νόμου, ὁ	law, custom
νόσος, νόσου, ἡ	disease, illness
νῦν	now
νύξ, νυκτός, ἡ	night

Ξ

ξένος, ξένου, ὁ	stranger, foreigner, host, guest, friend
ξίφος, ξίφους, τό	sword

Ο

ὁ, ἡ, τό	the
ὅδε, ἥδε, τόδε	this
ὁδός, ὁδοῦ, ἡ	road, path, way, journey
οἶδα	I know (*present, participle and infinitive only*)
οἰκέω	I live (in), inhabit, dwell
οἰκία, οἰκίας, ἡ	house, home
οἶνος, οἴνου, ὁ	wine
οἷός τ' εἰμί	I am able, can
ὀκτώ	eight
ὀλίγος, ὀλίγη, ὀλίγον	little
ὀλίγοι, ὀλίγαι ὀλίγα	few
ὄνομα, ὀνόματος, τό	name
ὅπλα, ὅπλων, τά	weapons, arms, armour
ὁράω, ὄψομαι, εἶδον, ὤφθην	I see
ὀργίζομαι, ὀργιοῦμαι, ὠργίσθην + dat.	I grow angry (with)
ὄρος, ὄρους, τό	mountain, hill

ὅς, ἥ, ὅ	who, which
ὅτι	that
οὐ, οὐκ, οὐχ	not
οὐδείς, οὐδεμία, οὐδέν	no-one, nothing, no
οὐδέποτε	never
οὔτε … οὔτε	neither … nor …
οὖν	therefore, and so
οὐρανός, οὐρανοῦ, ὁ	sky, heaven
οὗτος, αὕτη, τοῦτο	this
οὕτω(ς)	so, in this way

Π

παῖς, παιδός, ὁ and ἡ	child, son, daughter, boy, girl
πάλαι	long ago, in the past, formerly
παρά + acc.	contrary to, along, to
παρά + gen.	from (a person)
παρασκευάζω	I prepare
παρέχω	I provide, cause, produce
πᾶς, πᾶσα, πᾶν	all, every
πάσχω, πείσομαι, ἔπαθον	I suffer, experience
πατήρ, πατρός, ὁ	father
παύω	I stop
παύομαι (middle)	I stop, cease from (doing something)
πείθω	I persuade
πείθομαι, πείσομαι, ἐπιθόμην + dat.	I obey
πειράομαι, πειράσομαι	I try
πέμπτος, πέμπτη, πέμπτον	fifth
πέμπω	I send, escort
πέντε	five
περί + acc.	round
περί + gen.	about, concerning
πίνω, πιοῦμαι, ἔπιον	I drink
πίπτω, πεσοῦμαι, ἔπεσον	I fall
πιστεύω + dat.	I trust, believe
πιστός, πιστή, πιστόν	faithful, reliable
πλέω, πλεύσομαι, ἔπλευσα	I sail
πλήν	except
πλοῖον, πλοίου, τό	boat, cargo ship
πλούσιος, πλουσία, πλούσιον	rich

ποιέω	I do, make
ποῖος, ποία, ποῖον;	what sort of?
πόλεμος, πολέμου, ὁ	war
πολέμιοι, πολεμίων, οἱ	the enemy
πόλις, πόλεως, ἡ	city, state
πολίτης, πολίτου, ὁ	citizen
πολλάκις	often
πολύς, πολλή, πολύ	much
πολλοί, πολλαί, πολλά	many
πορεύομαι, πορεύσομαι, ἐπορεύθην	I travel, march
πόσος, πόση, πόσον;	how big? how much?
πόσοι, πόσαι, πόσα;	how many?
ποταμός, ποταμοῦ, ὁ	river
πότε;	when?
ποῦ;	where?
ποῖ;	to where?
πόθεν;	from where?
πούς, ποδός, ὁ	foot
πράσσω, πράξω, ἔπραξα, ἐπράχθην	I do, fare, manage
πρό + gen.	before, in front of
πρός + acc.	to, towards, against
προσβάλλω + dat.	I attack
πρότερον	before, formerly
πρῶτος, πρώτη, πρῶτον	first
πρῶτον	at first, first
πύλη, πύλης, ἡ	gate
πυνθάνομαι, πεύσομαι, ἐπυθόμην	I learn, ascertain, ask
πῦρ, πυρός, τό	fire
πῶς;	how?

Ρ

ῥᾴδιος, ῥᾳδία, ῥᾴδιον	easy

Σ

σιγή, σιγῆς, ἡ	silence
σῖτος, σίτου, ὁ	food, corn, bread
σοφός, σοφή, σοφόν	wise, clever
στρατηγός, στρατηγοῦ, ὁ	general, commander
στρατιά, στρατιᾶς, ἡ	army

στρατιώτης, στρατιώτου, ὁ	soldier
σύ	you
σός, σή, σόν	your
συλλέγω, συλλέξω, συνέλεξα	I collect, assemble
σύμμαχοι, συμμάχων, οἱ	allies
συμφορά, συμφορᾶς, ἡ	misfortune, disaster, event
σῴζω, σώσω, ἔσωσα, ἐσώθην	I save, keep, get away safely (*passive*)
σῶμα, σώματος, τό	body

T

ταχύς, ταχεῖα, ταχύ	fast, quick
... τε ... καί	both ... and
τεῖχος, τείχους, τό	wall
τέλος	end (adv. in the end), at last, finally,
τέσσαρες, τέσσαρες, τέσσαρα	four
τέταρτος, τετάρτη, τέταρτον	fourth
τιμάω	I honour, respect
τιμή, τιμῆς, ἡ	honour
τις, τι	(a) certain, someone, something
τίς; τί;	who? what? which?
τοιοῦτος, τοιαύτη, τοιοῦτο	such
τόπος, τόπου, ὁ	place
τοσουτος, τοσαυτη, τοσουτο	so great
τοσοῦτοι, τοσαῦται, τοσαῦτα	so many
τότε	then, at that time
τρεῖς, τρεῖς, τρία	three
τρέχω, δραμοῦμαι, ἔδραμον	I run
τρίτος, τρίτη, τρίτον	third
τύχη, τύχης, ἡ	chance, luck, fortune (good or bad)

Υ

ὕδωρ, ὕδατος, τό	water
υἱός, υἱοῦ, ὁ	son
ὕλη, ὕλης, ἡ	wood, forest
ὑμεῖς, ὑμῶν	you (*plural*)
ὑμέτερος, ὑμετέρα, ὑμέτερον	your
ὑπέρ + gen.	on behalf of
ὑπισχνέομαι, ὑποσχήσομαι, ὑπεσχόμην	I promise
ὕπνος, ὕπνου, ὁ	sleep

ὑπό + gen.	by (*with the agent of passive verbs*)
ὕστερον	later
ὑψηλός, ὑψηλή, ὑψηλόν	high

Φ

φαίνομαι, φανοῦμαι, ἐφάνην	I seem, appear
φέρω, οἴσω, ἤνεγκα, ἠνέχθην	I carry, bear, endure
φεύγω, φεύξομαι, ἔφυγον	I run away, flee, am accused, am banished
φημί, φήσω, ἔφην	I say
φιλέω	I love, like, am accustomed
φίλη, φίλης, ἡ	(female) friend
φίλος, φίλου, ὁ	(male) friend
φοβέομαι, φοβήσομαι, ἐφοβήθην	I am afraid, fear
φόβος, φόβου, ὁ	fear
φονεύω	I murder, kill
φύλαξ, φύλακος, ὁ	guard
φυλάσσω	I guard
φωνή, φωνῆς, ἡ	voice

Χ

χαλεπός, χαλεπή, χαλεπόν	difficult, dangerous, harsh
χειμών, χειμῶνος, ὁ	storm, winter
χείρ, χειρός, ἡ	hand
χράομαι, χρήσομαι, ἐχρησάμην + dat.	I use, treat
χρή (with acc. + infin.)	it is necessary
χρήματα, χρημάτων, τά	money, goods, property
χρήσιμος, χρησίμη, χρήσιμον	useful
χρόνος, χρόνου, ὁ	time
χρυσός, χρυσοῦ, ὁ	gold
χώρα, χώρας, ἡ	country, land

Ω

ὦ	o ... (addressing someone)
ὡς	when, as, because
ὡς τάχιστα	as quickly (etc.) as possible
ὥστε	that, so that, with the result that